Theological and Ideological Struggles

Two Cultures

at War

Jonathan Jang

Contents

Chapter1

Introduction

postle Paul introduces the battle faced by the Saints, saying, **"Finally, my brethren, be strong in the Lord, and in the power of his might. Put on the whole armour of God, that ye may be able to stand against the wiles of the devil. For we wrestle not against flesh and blood, but against principalities, against powers, against the rulers of the darkness of this world, against spiritual wickedness in high [places]. Wherefore take unto you the whole armour of God, that ye may be able to withstand in the evil day, and having done all, to stand."** (Ephesus6:10-13)

He says that the redeemed saints engage in spiritual battles. They have to stand against principalities, powers, the rulers of the darkness of this world, and the evil spirits in heaven. The first three are visible, whereas the last - invisible. In short, the evil spirits, invisible entities, reveal themselves through the world's visible things.

Apostle Paul says explicitly that these evil spirits now work among the sons of disobedience (Eph.2:2). They refer to the serpent's seed introduced in the Protoevangelium (Gen.3:15), while the sons of obedience - the woman's seed. As foretold in the original Gospel, the spiritual battle between them continues here in this world from the Fall to the present day.

God, the Creator, as Spirit, revealed Himself by having created the material world. Evil spirits also work, disguising themselves through worldly things. They are the ideas, philosophies, and values which oppose the faith in the Creator and develop into worldly customs and traditions. These are the objects for saints to fight. There are many slogans to wage these fights. However, there is no explanation on how to battle. Apostle Paul introduces it in detail.

An individual belief leads people to live life by judging and acting. It eventually determines a person's future and destiny. Then, what kind of belief is it? Religion is the base of every culture. It is because spirit necessarily flows into philosophy. Faith, therefore, is the sum of the thoughts, philosophy, and values accumulated in the person's mind (Mathew12:33-35).

And the religion comes split into two categories: faith in Creator and atheism, Creator and idolatry, or Jehovah and Baal. Regardless of the times, two kinds of beliefs have been a severe cause of the fights between ideas, philosophy, and values that always emerge in human society. This fight is both an ideological and spiritual battle.

Creation faith comes from the Primeval History of the Christian Bible (Genesis 1-11). By today's standards, the Primeval History looks like a myth. However, using the current mythical culture, the author had to record the History in the form of a tale for contemporary readers to understand.

There is no problem with the historicity of the original account. And it should have been orally handed down from generation to generation in a narrative form. The form was the best way of communicating with peoples in times of no letters.

The biblical historicity and narrative form of the Primeval

History tell how to interpret the Bible. The events, composed of the original History, have to be viewed as historical facts. And they are organically connected in the narrative with one another. Bible readers have to interpret the text with the help of the context.

The Primeval History of the Bible was the primitive history of universal humankind. It consists of only 11 chapters in the book of Genesis. A unique account of the chosen people followed it. The unique history was also one of the universal records of humanity.

The biblical author argues that the two narratives of Genesis are sufficient to reveal the future history of universal humankind. Christian theology should have paid particular attention to the primitive account, believing that God was the Bible's actual author.

Around the 2nd century AD, the apostolic era ended, and the church-father period began. The apostles of the New-Testamental times were Jews and well acquainted with the Old Testament. However, the church fathers were Gentiles and more familiar with Plato and Aristoteles than Moses.

In those days, Greek culture dominated the Roman Empire. The Rabbinical Jews had already translated the Old Testament into Greek. Furthermore, the Apostles had written the New Testament also in Greek. The fathers interpreted biblical Scriptures on not Hebrew culture but Greek culture to help people understand the Bible.

In 313 AD, Christianity became the state religion of the

Byzantine Empire. The Roman Empire, which had persecuted Christianity, became her guardian and turned into a Byzantine Empire. Christianity, which should distinguish herself from the world, married the world's regime. Accordingly, the Greek culture began to dominate Christian theology.

European theology much more preferred the New Testament to the Old Testament. The Old Testament God is the deity of war, and the New Testament God is the God of love. And while the Old Testament God is a low-level god who created the material world, the New Testament God is a high-level god who revealed the spiritual world.

The Christian theology in Europe enjoyed emphasizing the redemption from the material world. Therefore, European theology originally started from the Fall (Gen. 3), not from the Creation (Gen. 1-2). And it began to assert an alternative theology that the Europeans replaced the Jews. Thus, the Hellenistic theology utterly neglected the Primeval History inclusive of the Creation Article. It was mainly due to the dualism of Greek philosophy.

The ignorance of the Old Testament, in its turn, pushed the European theologians to ignore the Primeval History that recorded the first universal history of humanity. It was a too fatal mistake. The Christian Bible starts with the Primeval History, which begins with the story of Creation.

The start of biblical Creation looks forward to its end and also the process between them. Accordingly, the Creation Article's ignorance results in the loss or lack of theological direction and ideological goal. Christianity of that kind became one of the worldly religions, and Christian theology fell into religious studies.

It was the unfortunate result of abandoning the teachings and lessons from the Primeval History, including Creation's story. History also deals with the universal humankind, who always left the belief in God, the Creator. And again, History reveals how the future of universal humanity will unfold. Unfortunately, European Christianity disregarded the ideas, philosophy, and values of the Bible.

Nowadays, the ideological side of the world is wholly oppositive to Biblical Creationism. International human society, losing order, is collapsing every day. The global chaos and darkness are the misfortunate result of having abandoned both creation theology and faith.

Satan always secretly works to destruct the Divine Creation's belief and aims for social confusion and darkness through ideological division. For this, he nowadays acts among the sons of disobedience covertly. Naturally, spirituality flows into ideology. Even today continues the spiritual struggle between the woman's seed and the serpent's seed, prophesied in the Protoevangelium (Genesis3:15).

The Christian church must return to the Primeval History's creative theology and revive its theological teachings. It is because the Primeval History provides biblical ideas, philosophy, and values for human society to pursue and realize happiness.

Chapter 2

God's Eternal Decrees

C hristian Bible starts with the Creation Article (Genesis 1-2). The Divine creation is the excellence and superiority of the Bible so that other religions lack. True religion should tell about the origin of all things.

The Creator is Elohim, omnipotent God. God's creation, an invisible spiritual entity, made it possible for all visible things to exist. Thus, the Bible presupposes God, the Creator, and his spiritual existence. This premise does not allow atheists to participate in the debate about God's presence.

The biblical creation (Genesis 1-2) logically presupposes a plan and purpose, set by the Creator before the world's foundation. It is because action follows a plan. God's Decrees are another name of the project and goal. It is a prerequisite to know about God's Decrees to study His Creation.

The creation story was the starting point for the rest of the Bible. The study of the Divine Decrees helps to see the goal and direction of biblical Creation. The purpose and direction serve as a guide for the Bible interpretation.

Unfortunately, it is difficult to find specific revelations of God's intention in the Old Testament. Surprisingly enough, it is easy to see God's Decrees in the New Testament. They are not just the aim of soteriology.

1.   **God, First Cause:** Rome 11:36

Apostle Paul introduces God, the Redeemer as follows:

"For of him, and through him, and to him, [are] all things: to whom [be] glory forever. Amen." (Rome11:36)

All things are the result of God's Creation. Naturally, all things came from the Lord, develop through Him, and finally return unto Him. The Master directs all: departure, development, and arrival. The purpose, already revealed in the beginning, will be achieved at the end through the course of evolution.

What was the starting by the Lord? It was the ministry of Divine Creation. This work followed pre-planning. Likewise, all the Divine ministries recorded in the Bible were nothing but a process and result of the plan, predetermined by the Master. Pre-planning focused on what to do, that is, an abstract strategy. However, the Divine ministries concentrated on how to do, that is, concrete tactics.

Apostle Paul was very good at having embodied the Divine Decrees as the Holy Triune God's ministries. In this way, the Decrees became eternal ones. The Primeval History, recorded from the 1st chapter unto the 11th of the Book of Genesis, historically explained the eternal Decrees. At the same time, the Primeval History told about the history of universal humanity. The diagram below well illustrates the relationship between them.

Bible		Eph.1:4-6	Gen.1-11	Revelation
event	content	Predestination	Primeval History	rejection
	mattered	God, the Father	Pre-incarnational Christ	Post-incarnational Christ
	meaning	Pre-planning	Creation/Fall	End
God		from	Through	Unto
Christology		Pre-incarnational		Post-incarnational
nature		what to do	How to do	

2. **Predestination and election**: Ephesus 1: 4-6

"According as he hath chosen us in him before the foundation of the world, that we should be holy and without blame before him in love: Having predestinated us unto the adoption of children by Jesus Christ to himself, according to the good pleasure of his will, To the praise of the glory of his grace, wherein he hath made us accepted in the beloved."(Eph.1:4-6)

The interpretation of this text is as the chart below.

		Predestination	Election
object		Special group	
time		Before creation	
basis		Father's good pleasure	Christ
way		Jesus Christ	Father's love
traitor		abstract	Concrete
military		Eternal strategy	Dispensational tactics
Christology		Jesus Christ	Christ
target	1st	adoption	holiness
	2nd	To the praise of the glory of His grace	
aim	practical	God's family	God's Kingdom
	theoretical	What to do	How to do

a. **Father's predestination**

The main verb is to elect in the Greek text, while an auxiliary verb - to predestinate. And according to Greek grammar, the act of predestination precedes the act of election in the tense. In short, the predestination before the election. The predestination is an abstract plan, while the election is concrete action. Time conception well explains the theological meaning. In the Bible, history already demonstrates logic very well.

The good pleasure of Divine will is the basis for

predestination. So, predestination is God's happy will. No one can stop or break the joyful will of the omnipotent God. Predestination will be indeed fulfilled and consummated in history. Therefore, the Divine predestination denies deism from the beginning. Moreover, God is perfect goodness, righteousness, and love itself. Being determines the content of doing because doing depends upon being.

The goal of Divine predestination was to adopt a particular group as the sons of God. The adoption will be possible through Jesus Christ. A specific group was an object of love, according to the joyful Divine will. God will always be pleased with the object. All-powerful and covenant-faithful God will indeed adopt this group through Christ, the Son of God. The grace of adoption comes from the good pleasure of God's will forever.

Father's Decrees will realize themselves through Jesus Christ. For this, God the Father had given birth to Christ as God the Son. The Son, knowing Father's wish, will gladly devote oneself to the Father. Without the Son, no way to adopt a particular group to the sons of God. God the Son was the only mediator for the group before the creation of the world.

The expression 'through Jesus Christ' does not necessarily presuppose the Fall of humanity. The work of Christ's mediation is always essential on both sides of God and a particular group. If the predestination comes from the good pleasure of God's will, the adoption will surely come true through Jesus Christ historically.

The predestination will undoubtedly result in the adoption. Why was the word of son used? Sons mean the children, as members of the family. The eventual result will lie in setting up God's own family. God will be their Father, Christ will be the Firstborn (Rom. 8:29, Hebrews 1:6), and a specific group will be his brothers and Father's sons.

When the members increase in number, the Divine family will expand its scope and become a society. When it further broadens the size of a community, the family will eventually become God's Kingdom. To build the kingdom of God will be the ultimate goal of predestination. It is well understandable by common sense. A lot of families make up a society, and various organizations consist of a country. Apostle Paul, deliberately borrowing the word son, tries to explain the purpose of predestination.

In conclusion, the Divine predestination reveals that God the Father will deliver heavenly blessings to a specific group in the form of God's kingdom with the Holy Spirit's help. All of it will come out of God's joyful will. To belong to God's family or the kingdom of God will be the supreme blessings for humankind. There, He will rule as the Head. The kingdom of God will be an eternal paradise.

b. **Father's election**

Father's abstract predestination necessarily needs His concrete act of election. God's election is His other plan concretely to realize the predestination. The timing, condition, and goal of God's choice are apparent in His election.

The time of God's selection was before creation. God favored a particular group in advance before birth. The Divine choice had nothing to do with their merit. Father's election directly opposes the doctrines such as foreknowledge and justification by law. According to God's Decrees, the group already existed in Christ before birth or in eternity.

Before creation, the particular group had already received the unconditional, one-sided, and irrevocable grace of election according to God's will's good pleasure. Its only condition was in Christ. The expression 'in Christ' also presupposes 'Out of Christ.' The group out of Christ is the object of abandonment, utterly devoid of God's grace of election.

Apostle Paul insists on the doctrine of double predestination. However, from a human's point of view, it is quite impossible to know who is the object of election or abandonment. It is entirely impossible to judge whether or not God elects a specific person. That kind of controversy is something like usurping God's authority.

The goal of choice lies in that a particular group will become holy and blameless before God in His love. Holiness before God means that a saint will reach the glorification level where he no longer can sin. Citizens who will live in God's Kingdom must be holy and unblemished children like God the Father (Matthew 5:48).

Only the love of God will enable saints to acquire and reach this perfect status. In conclusion, the grace of God's choice will be possible only in Christ, and the love of God will lead saints to reach the glorification level. In other words, the purpose of divine predestination will be reachable through Jesus Christ, while the goal of God's election - in the love of God. God's love means the grace of God's perseverance.

c. **The ultimate goal of predestination and election**

The election logically follows and depends on predestination. The election aims at the glorification of saints, while predestination – at their acquisition of sonship. Both goals have the same theological meaning. The chosen in Christ by God before creation will gain the sonship by the faith in Jesus Christ someday after the Creation, and grow in the love of God finally to become glorious sons, holy and blameless before God. Father's Decrees already well explain the order of salvation.

By the Son's and the Holy Spirit's works, a specific group will finally become the glorious sons before God, according to the predestination and election of God the Father. They will be the members of God's family and the citizens of God's Kingdom. This status will be the supreme glory given in the form of the kingdom of God. This glory is glorification itself and, at the same time, means heavenly blessings.

Apostle Paul says that God, the Father, will impart the heavenly blessings through belonging or relationship. Only a normal relationship with God makes it possible to belong to the family and the kingdom where God is the Head and Ruler. God is forever good and righteous. The members of God's family and the citizens of the kingdom will be happy forever.

The Divine Decrees teach that God's kingdom should be the primary theme until the end of the Bible. The final entry into the kingdom of God will be possible in Christ, through Jesus Christ, with the help of God the Spirit, and in the love of God the Father. All these blessings always come from the good pleasure of God's will. In its turn, saints give heartful thanks, praises, and honor to God the Father. It will be the ultimate purpose of faith life by saints.

So far, the doctrines of theology, Christology, and soteriology have been under careful examination from God's Eternal Decrees. All they, being organically connected, aim toward the doctrine of God's Kingdom. It means that systematic theology, having nothing to do with God's Kingdom, loses the meaning and direction of their existence. It is because God's Kingdom is the strategic purpose of His Eternal Decrees.

Here is one important conclusion. The Divine Decrees, set before the world's creation, will surely come true after the world's foundation. The Divine plan means that Christ, the Son of God, will work at the times already determined by God. The predestination and election of God the Father are also absolutely dominated by the concept of time. Therefore, God's Eternal Decrees also have an eschatological character.

3. **The ministries of the Holy Triune God:** Ephesus1:4-14

The Almighty Deity first revealed Himself as the Creator. Thus, the act of Creation (Genesis 1-2) was God's first ministry. The first ministry was the start, the foundation, and the basis of the other Divine works. In this respect, the Creation article provides the principle to interpret the rest of the biblical texts.

Creation, like a secret code, is the key to Bible interpretation. The reason is that the creation record shares the purpose of eternal decrees. The difference in time between before and after God's creation makes no difference in the goal.

Apostle Paul records all the Holy Triune God's works in one Greek sentence (Ephesians 1:3-14): the predestination and election of God the Father, the Redemption, and Lordship of God the Son, the sealing and guarantee of God the Holy Spirit.

	God the Father	God the Son	God the Spirit
ministry	Predestination /Election	Redemption /Lordship	Sealing /Guarantee
meaning	Pre-planning	Fulfillment/ consummation	Deliverance/ application
time	Before Creation	After Creation	
goal	God's Kingdom		
God's family	Plan to adopt	adoption	inheritance
Order of	Glorification	Justification	Sanctification

salvation			
Cause	Good pleasure of Divine will	Father's love	

Father's Decrees - predestination and election - will come into historical realization by the Son's and the Holy Spirit's works. The methods of Their ministries differ from time to time. However, all the goals of Their careers are to achieve the Divine purpose of the eternal Decrees. The different ministries of the Holy Trinity, sharing the same goal, will finally reach the Father's objective.

The Divine Decrees provide a strategy for the ministries by the Son and the Holy Spirit, respectively. On the other hand, the Son's and the Holy Spirit's works are tactics coming out of the strategy. Accordingly, the Son and the Holy Spirit's tactical goals will fulfill Father's abstract strategy after Creation. Readers need precisely to interpret the tactics of the Son and the Spirit according to the Father's plan.

The study of the Father's ministry - predestination and election – offers fundamental knowledge of God's strategy. This knowledge reveals the strategic direction and goal of the tactical ministries by the Son and the Holy Spirit. It also helps to know what the tactical objective of the Divine Creation is. In other words, the detailed examination of God's predestination and election makes it possible to know the tactical goal of the biblical text subject to a specific redemptive history.

"Blessed [be] the God and Father of our Lord Jesus Christ, who hath blessed us with all spiritual blessings in heavenly [places] in Christ: " (Eph.1:3)

Apostle Paul writes a song of glory immediately after finishing his greeting of the 1st chapter of Ephesus's book. God's blessings received by the saints are so great. Their character is unique. God the Father gives in Christ the blessings, both heavenly and Spiritual. It is because the Father imparts them through the Holy Spirit to the elect in Christ the Son.

Immediately, Paul records the works of the Holy Trinity God. This blessing will be embodied and distributed to the saints by the work of the Holy Triune God. First, the Father determined these blessings by His Predestination and Election before creating the world (Eph.1:4-6). The benefits came into historical fulfillment with the Redemption and Lordship of the Son (verses 7-12). Nowadays, the Holy Spirit's seal and guarantee help saints enjoy these blessings now on earth (verses 13-14).

The blessings start with the Father. Father is the source of all gifts. The Son's and the Holy Spirit's works make the saints enjoy these blessings even in this world. It is why the study of the Divine Decrees - Predestination and Election – is significant and critical for interpreting the ministries of God the Son and God the Holy Spirit.

Chapter 3

Primeval History

The Bible's Primeval History (Genesis 1-11) first shows God's will and wish to realize the Eternal Decrees after creation. It is why the primitive narrative is not a myth and cannot take it lightly. The actual history reveals, for the first time, what God wants from humankind. Thus, this biblical history provides the principles that generally govern the life of universal humanity.

The relationship between God's Eternal Decrees and Primeval History is similar to that of Greek philosophy between ideal and phenomenon. The former revealed itself through the latter. However, the second cannot complete the first. Plato, the Greek philosopher, argued this. On the other hand, Aristotle emphasized the phenomenon, claiming that he could not fully recognize Plato's ideal world.

Plato oriented his interest in philosophical thinking, while Aristotle - in a scientific review. The reason was the ideal method for both thoughts. On the contrary, the Christian Bible holds both of them according to the logical precedence. First, God, the Creator, showed ideal through phenomenon by the Divine act of Creation. Next, the latter will enter the former by the holy act of Redemption. Thus, the Bible will eventually overcome the Greek dualism.

Contrary to our expectation, however, the original History always showed human society's betrayal behavior against God the Creator. Each time, God intervened in human history and secretly worked to attain the purpose of creation at His appointed time. The creative goal is also the purpose of the Eternal Decrees. Without His intervention, human society would always be in confusion and darkness.

The book of Genesis records the Primeval history from the 1st chapter until the 11th. And the history of the chosen nation from the 12th chapter follows the Primeval History. Therefore, the first history is the root and beginning of the latter narrative. It means that the previous history cannot separate itself from early history.

Primeval history goes into two eras of Creation and Fall. The age of the Fall has two periods of Pre-Flood and Post-Flood. The Pre-Flood era divides itself into the periods by following comparisons: Cain and Abel, Cain and Seth, and the sons of God and the daughters of men. And the Post-Flood era is divided into the following: Noah as a type of second Adam, Nimrod as a type of anti-Christ, and Babel Tower as a culmination of men's betrayal.

God the Son created the universe and everything in it to realize the pre-creational Decrees of God the Father (Ephesians 1:4-6). This way, God, the Creator, expressed the love and grace of the Father toward humankind. However, humanity rejected the Father by disobeying the Son (Genesis 3-11).

The Fall article was divided into two parts: personal and social disobedience. The first disobedience refers to the Fall by

Adam and the murder by Cain. Adam was the representative of humanity, while Cain was his descendant. On the other hand, the second disobedience means the social depravities: the mixed marriage between the godly and ungodly, and the incident of Babel Tower by Noah's descendants. In such a way, universal humanity gradually came to corruption.

According to the Father's Predestination and Election, the Creation Article (Genesis 1-2) first reveals what God wanted to do. However, the Fall articles (Genesis 3-11) records how God worked from time to time against disobedient humanity. In short, the Creation article revealed God's strategy, but the Fall articles - His tactics, respectively.

1.   **God's Creation:** Genesis 1-2 chapters

Common sense says that action follows a plan. Naturally, the Divine act of Creation followed God's Eternal Decrees. There were tactical differences in time between them, but there was no strategic difference in sharing a common final goal. Likewise, there were both continuity and discontinuity between the first and second chapters of the book of Genesis.

Genesis	1st chapter	2nd chapter
God's name	Omnipotent God/ Elohim	Covenant God/ Jehovah
creation	cosmic	earthly
times	Six days	Sixth day
Main theme	God's Kingdom/ rule	good and evil tree/ law

humanity	identity	Created in God's image	Holder of God's breadth
	Man/woman	Horizontal	Vertical
	living	In society	In family
mission		Cultural mandate	Keeping covenant
God's Kingdom		celestial	earthly
aim		Strategic goal	Tactical targets

Genesis chapter 1 records human creation and cultural mission (Genesis 1:26-28) with God's creation in the cosmic background (Genesis 1:1-25). It seemed to support heliocentrism with the sun at the celestial center. On the other hand, Genesis chapter 2 focuses on human creation (Genesis2:7) and creative covenant (Genesis2:17) to establish and expand God's Kingdom in human society. It seemingly supported geocentrism with the earth at the cosmic center.

God's unchangeable strategic objective in Chapter 1 was to construct the kingdom of God (Genesis 1:26). However, His tactical targets in Chapter 2 was how to carry His strategic objective out (Genesis 2:17). Chapter 1 revealed the strategic intent, while Chapter 2 - tactical methods.

In terms of Deity, God of chapter 1 was Elohim, the almighty God, while God of chapter 2 - Jehovah, the covenant God. And in terms of man, the person of chapter 1 was like God's son in His glorious image (Genesis 1:27), gaining rulership on behalf of the Creator (Genesis 1:26-28). However, the man of Chapter

2 was a humble being of the earth (Genesis 2:7), but an amazing being enough to sign a covenant with the Creator equally (Genesis 2:17).

In Chapter 1, Adam and Eve were the executors of the cultural mission as servants of God, having a vertical relationship with the Creator. However, in Chapter 2, Adam represented humankind as a covenant partner equal to the Creator, having a horizontal relationship with Him. These are theology and anthropology of the Creation record (Genesis 1-2).

Both Genesis 1 and 2 record that humans could exist thanks to God's creative actions. However, there remained an apparent difference in identity between them. Adam and Eve were under Elohim as His servants in chapter 1, but Adam - with Jehovah as an equal covenant partner in chapter 2.

It is the theological doctrine of anthropology from the creative perspective. Christ, the Son of God, was the Creator. Under Elohim and with Jehovah, these Old-Testamental expressions can replace the New-Testamental ones, in Christ, and with Christ.

a.   **Cosmic Creation**: Genesis 1

The Creation record of the 1st and 2nd chapter of Genesis tells the origin and beginning of all things. This story is the excellence of the Christian Bible. This excellence is natural. Creator, as God, is the object of faith. God must first reveal Himself so that humans, as the subject of religion, could believe in Him.

The Christian Bible introduces that God is the Creator. Only the Creator makes all things possible to exist. The universe and nature, as well as humankind, were His creations. The Creator is the Lord of lords, King of kings. The Creator is the only God.

The act of Creation logically implies that the Creator already had a plan and purpose in advance. And everything created is in the process of existence, preservation, and maintenance according to the target of Divine Creation.

However, Greek philosophy regards the Creation article as a myth that has nothing to do with history. And it neglects the Creator of the material world. But the Bible authors wrote Genesis like a myth under their contemporary culture. It was to help the concurrent people understand the Creation story well.

Myth conveys meaning without fact. It is like a theory. The Bible's Creation article looks like a myth, but it gives theological implications together with historical facts. The Creation narrative is needed only to say the action, purpose, and sense of God's Creation. There was no need to explain how scientifically to create the cosmic world in the mythical era. It is irrational to criticize and judge that the creation records of the Bible are unscientific.

. **Eschatological world**: Genesis 1:1

"In the beginning, God created the heavens and the earth." (Genesis 1:1)

The 1st verse of the 1st chapter of Genesis, the 1st book of the Bible, proclaimed God's Creation of the universe and Earth, nature, and humankind, saying that the Creator was the only God.

This verse was the background of the six-day creation and the starting point of the Primeval History. Shortly speaking, God's act of Creation was the starting point of the whole Bible. It is impossible to interpret the Bible without the starting point. The New Testament is no exception in it.

The above scripture declared God's action of Creation on the first day as a historical fact. Also, the 1st-day Creation provided a fundamental background for the outcomes over the remaining five days. In other words, the outcomes were the result of the 1st-day creation. Everything was not a coincidence but a product of inevitability.

Everything in the universe and nature came to live according to the Creator's plan and purpose. Thanks to it, all things had the purpose and meaning of existence. Only belief in the creation story of the Bible as history could find all kinds of answers to all philosophical questions about life, the universe, and nature.

In this respect, Hebraic thought is superior to Greek thought. It is very natural that every country and nation, having accepted the Christian Gospel based on Hebraic ideology, is bound to improve or reform in all fields of its society better than ever.

People do what they believe. What will the belief in God's creation bring forth? The Creation articles give fundamental lessons about the Creator, the world, and life. The lessons reform a thinking frame and the way of thinking or behaving accordingly.

The word **"beginning"** refers to the first time (John1:1). At that time, God created space together with the material world: the cosmic universe and the natural world. The celestial bodies occupy space. Shortly speaking, when time started, space and material also began to exist together.

Two teachings are available. First, time precedes space. And next, the beginning of the created time logically presupposes its end, as well. In short, protology is eschatology. Time created by God had an eschatological meaning and concept.

Protology always aims for eschatology. It means that the first will be fulfilled or consummated by the second. The previous is characteristically terrestrial, whereas the latter - heavenly. In other words, the former takes the form of prophecy and revelation, while the latter - the shape of fulfillment and consummation, respectively. The Old Testament, therefore, focuses on the protology, but the New Testament - on the eschatology.

The Creator began to create all things according to the already-planned purpose. Time will come to an end when God fully achieve His own goal. At the same time, all items of the cosmic world will terminate their existence. The beginning and the end of time also mean the first beginning and the last ending of the material world. The Bible testifies to this.

"Who hath wrought and done [it], calling the generations from the beginning? I the LORD, the first, and with the last; I [am] he." (Isa. 41:4)

"I am Alpha and Omega, the beginning and the ending, saith the Lord, which is, and which was, and which is to come, the Almighty." (Rev.1:8)

"And he said unto me, it is done. I am Alpha and Omega, the beginning and the end. I will give unto him that is athirst of the fountain of the water of life freely." (Rev.21:6)

"I am Alpha and Omega, the beginning and the end, the first and the last." (Rev.22:13)

The Bible's creation story (Genesis 1-2) teaches that time precedes and dominates space and material. The time plan of God's Creation is not only physical but also theological. The creation plan and its achievement were by God's schedule. With this schedule, all things were and will be in existence, preservation, and maintenance.

The Christian Bible emphasizes that time is fundamentally more important than space. The Bible advises human society to live not with the mind and concept of space, but with the sense and idea of time.

"Of old hast thou laid the foundation of the Earth: and the heavens [are] the work of thy hands. They shall perish, but thou shalt endure: yea, all of them shall wax old like a garment; as a vesture shalt thou change them, and they shall be changed: But thou [art] the same, and thy years shall have no end. The children of thy servants shall continue, and their seed shall be established before thee." (Psalm 102:25-28)

Denial of the belief in God's creation, in its turn, causes people to ignore these fundamental teachings of the Biblical Creation. First of all, the Creator is invisible. Time cannot be sensed and felt by the human body. On the other hand, the created world is visible. You see nature as a physical object of conquest. Besides, you believe yourself as the master of your own life.

The common sense of the visible world always makes you more obsessed with the idea of space than that of time. You live your life according to the way of thinking based on the concept of space. However, the biblical narrative of God's Creation implies an end to all things of this cosmic world. And from the beginning of time, the end had already been set by God.

It, however, could not come soon. God's purpose of creation will be fulfilled and consummated according to the schedule. In this process, God repeatedly sent prophets to foretell and warn about the future end.

The plan and work of God's Creation are the works of Almighty God himself. And the fulfillment and consummation of these works will be possible only by God the Creator. Humans cannot complete these works. The Creator continues to reveal His omnipotence and integrity, always keeping in His mind the creation purpose's achievement. Accordingly, the Creator as Spirit will inevitably incarnate into a human.

"Who hath delivered us from the power of darkness, and hath translated [us] into the kingdom of his dear Son: In whom we have redemption through his blood, [even] the forgiveness of sins: Who is the image of the invisible God, the firstborn of every creature: For by him were all things created, that are in heaven, and that are in Earth, visible and invisible, whether [they be] thrones, or dominions, or principalities, or powers: all things were created by him, and for him: And he is before all things, and by him all things consist. And he is the head of the body, the church: who is the beginning, the firstborn from the dead; that in all [things] he might have the preeminence." (Col1:13-18)

The creation of all things implies the completion of the purpose as well as the process of completion. Logically, departure presupposes arrival as well as the process between them. All of these follow God's pre-planned schedule. In this respect, the Creation Article (Genesis 1-2) is an essential eschatological revelation, too.

Humanity, who ignores the faith of creation, favors thinking and living dominated by the visible space and material world more than the invisible God and the insensible time. As a result, space and matter dominate human society ideologically.

What is the end of this society? The denial of the faith in creation pushes people to value clothing more than the body and food more than life (Matthew 6:25). Wealth and riches are everything. They seek and enjoy temporal wealth and material prosperity. Their freedom and hedonism gradually degrade human society in terms of ethics and morality, collapses it from the inside, and eventually destroys itself.

But what about a society dominated by faith in God the Creator? The belief helps people live with the concept of time. Consciously or unconsciously, the idea of time governs the human way of thinking. God's spiritual teachings clothe themselves with the history and culture of human society. In that way, people lead eschatological life. The practice of thinking by time helps their social life meet God's creation purpose. Freedom is controllable by a higher level of civilization.

In this eschatological life, theology cannot separate itself from human society. Man is a spiritual and social being and, at the same time, an instinctive and economic animal. The material world continually changes together with time. Knowing this, the godly man always tries to make his thinking less dominated by space and material. They don't worry about useless wealth and temporary prosperity.

"From men [which are] thy hand, O LORD, from men of the world, [which have] their portion in [this] life, and whose belly thou fillest with thy hid [treasure]: they are full of children, and leave the rest of their [substance] to their babes. As for me, I will behold thy face in righteousness: I shall be satisfied, when I awake, with thy likeness." (Psalm17:14-15)

"Lay not up for yourselves treasures upon earth, where moth and rust doth corrupt, and where thieves break through and steal: But lay up for yourselves treasures in heaven, where neither moth nor rust doth corrupt, and where thieves do not break through nor steal: For where your treasure is, there will your heart be also." (Matt6:19-21)

"And he spake a parable unto them, saying, the ground of a certain rich man brought forth plentifully: And he thought within himself, saying, what shall I do, because I have no room where to bestow my fruits? And he said, this will I do: I will pull down my barns, and build greater; and there will I bestow all my fruits and my goods. And I will say to my soul, Soul, thou hast much goods laid up for many years; take thine ease, eat, drink, [and] be merry. But God said unto him, [Thou] fool, this night thy soul shall be required of thee: then whose shall those things be, which

thou hast provided? So [is] he that layeth up treasure for himself, and is not rich toward God." (Luk12:16-21)

Genesis 1:1 teaches that time dominates space and matter. The concept of created time is the basis of Christian thoughts, philosophy, and values. From the start, time always flows and advances toward its arrival and ending through the process between them.

In the end, the scriptures mentioned above insist on a linear view of human history and the world.

. **Periodic World**: Genesis 1:1-31

The Creation Article (Genesis 1-2) shows how God created the world. God's action of Creation already implies the first beginning and last ending of this world. God decided them in the purpose and project of God's Creation. However, there remains only one question: when will be the ending time?

The creation record teaches a linear view of history that goes straight from departure to arrival. Like this, human history and society also continue to run from the starting point of creation toward the ending one. It is the Hebraic view of history based on Biblical Creationism. However, God's Creation also provides a different view of history.

God had performed the works of Creation for six days. God created the original universe, supernatural light, and time on the

1st day (verses 1-5), the sky on the 2nd day (verses 6-8), sea and land (ground) on the 3rd day (verses 9-13), the sun, the moon, and the stars on the 4th day (verses 14-19), the beasts of the sky and the sea on the 5th day (verses 20-23), and the animals, living things, and humans on the 6th day (verses 24-31).

The six-day Creation consists of two groups: the first three-day creation and the second three-day one. God's creative act shows periodicity.

	1st three days	2nd three days
1st day	The original universe, time, and supernatural light	Sun, moon, and stars (natural light)
2nd day	firmament	Animals of heaven and sea
3rd day	Land, sea, and ground plants	Land beasts, insects, and Human
goal	Habitat	Habitants

In the first three days, the habitat made its first appearance from the original universe, and in the second three days, inhabitants began to settle and live there. God's act of Creation showed both repetition and development: where to reside preceded who to reside.

It shows repetition and development between the first and fourth days, the second and fifth days, and the third and sixth days. The Divine actions of Creation had periodically developed.

As God's work repeats itself, so it develops and advances.

The creative periodicity was extraordinarily rational and scientific. It means that God, the Creator, will work in the future in the same way as He had created. This creative periodicity was explained by the Dutch theologian 'Geerhardus Voss' as biblical revelations' gradualism.

First, God does what He wants, and then He gives revelation about it. God's works and biblical revelations are very close to each other. The graduality of biblical revelations argues that, like God's Creation, God's acts and words repeat the same topic and develop it better than ever.

The eschatological view of history seemingly insists on development without repetition. There is no continuity between past and present and between present and future. However, the Bible's periodic Creation insists that revelations do not suddenly develop into a new logic, as if the new one has nothing to do with the former one.

Humankind, as God's only companionship, cannot comprehend any present revelation disconnected from the past one. There is no way to interpret the present without the past. Naturally, the redemptive history in the Bible repeatedly developed with its past on the basis.

God, the Creator, is eternally self-existing. The past, present, and future are like a sight for Him. God works unchangingly from time to time to achieve the same purpose. Because the purpose and plan of God's creation already included and determined its departure and arrival and the process between them.

It is why biblical revelations develop over and over again. And in the history of God's kingdom, He uses many different tactical aims to achieve a strategic goal. Various tactical objectives always contribute to the achievement of one strategic objective.

Biblical revelations repeatedly reflect God's strategy and tactics. So, God's words show the continuity and discontinuity between the past, present, and future. Continuity means repetition of theological meaning, but discontinuity - its historical development.

The biblical view of history is different from the circular view of history, supported by Greek philosophy that emphasizes endless repetition. The Greek idea of history has no eschatological meaning and concept.

The Bible's view of history is a linear view of history, which continues directly to run toward the end. However, the Bible's Creation article also insists on periodical development. Christian Bible, therefore, declares a spiral view of history and the world. As the environment and conditions change over time, so history and culture newly form. God works in a new age in an enhanced way.

Even at this time, God's tactical goals go toward the achievement of the strategic target. It is why the redemptive history or secular history always shows both repetition and development: continuity and discontinuity. In this way, they will finally come to an end.

Biblical Creation article teaches two things about time. Time and space always go together. Time changes the natural environment and conditions. However, they are still dependent on time. Time is a concept above space and matter.

The material world, as the inhabitant of space, advances, being subject to straight-going time. The world cannot resist the passage of time. The Creation Article teaches humanity a lesson that the temporal way of thinking is more important than the spatial pattern of thinking.

The temporal way of thinking advises humanity to approach the universe, nature, humankind, and history with the concept of time. The Creation record teaches that the idea of time is fundamental to biblical beliefs, philosophy, and values.

In the spiral change of time, the world and history repeat their appearance periodically but always develop simultaneously. As a result, the past, present, and future are close to one another but become differently better.

Three tenses are similar in meaning and, at the same time, different in their duty. It is necessary to distinguish between their continuity and discontinuity over time. Thus, the spiral view of history is instrumental in interpreting the Bible and the world.

Redemptive or secular history, always repeating itself, develops toward completion. Like living things, they grow daily for existence. The existentialist likes to judge the past by the already-developed present. It does not fit at all with the spiral view of history.

Today, people think that the Bible belongs to culture as far behind the present time. They discard the Bible like an old book. However, even historians say that understanding the past is the only way to know the present. Even today, the Bible is still needed.

Mature humans think, reason, and judge the changing world and human society with two concepts: repetition and development. While looking at the present, it is possible to discover what has developed. Repetition says that the present is the result of the past. And development advises against judging the past as the present.

Regretfully enough, human society prefers the concept of space to that of time. What is now visible more appeals to humankind than what is invisible. It is always obsessed with the material world, visual today. They need only the spatial way of thinking, which usually depends upon reason.

Bible teaches that it is better to choose a temporal way of thinking, but not a spatial pattern of thinking. The former will be an excellent choice only when there is faith in the Creator. Only time mindset recommends us to look at the present together with the past and future.

After all, spatial thinking is a closed way of thinking, but temporal reasoning - open one. The former sees only the present world, but the latter considers the world to come, too. Furthermore, the first provides an optimistic or hedonistic view of history and society, but the second - a pessimistic or ascetic one.

However, the spiral view of history, asserted by the Bible, recommends both of them. This world and history repeatedly move forward towards the catastrophe of the end. On the other hand, the end means the perfect achievement of the purpose of Creation for God. Until this end, God's created world will continue to exist, showing repetition and development.

Today the concept of space governs the ideas, philosophy, and values of human society. Human society always misunderstands that the material world, occupying space, exists forever. It is a temptation that continually tests human society. Denial of the belief in the Creator leads to this temptation.

The Creation Article (Genesis 1-2) asserts that all things are not the result of chance. All things inevitably exist according to the will and purpose of the Creator. Saints have faith that helps them interpret everything according to the will of the Creator, but not according to common sense and reason.

In this respect, the world's study is nothing more than elementary education (Gal. 4:3). The laws, keeping the universe and nature in stable motion, are objects of science. Science pushes people to judge all things by common sense or reason.

However, God the Creator, having determined the natural law for all existing things, implanted it in the universe and nature toward the purpose of God's Creation. It is why humanity cannot live with reason alone.

"Through faith, we understand that the worlds were framed by the word of God so that things which are seen were not made of things which do appear." (Hebrews 11:3).

The biblical Creation teaches us to choose a spiral view of history, including both the historical views, linear and circular. So, a mature believer shouldn't be biased towards either. He lives his own life on the way of thinking, not by space but by time.

. **Body-like World:** Genesis 1:1-25

Genesis 1 has two divided contents in itself: the creation of all-natural things in the universe (verses 1-25) and the creation of humans (verses 26-31). The first was the creation of impersonal nature, and the second was the creation of a personal being.

The first was the creation of space and nature, and the second was that of humans, who would act on Earth. The former was the stage for the latter. However, the latter originates from the previous. Both of them are close together. In the end, the Creation article recorded a world where humanity should work. The Creation article directly opposes Hellenistic dualism.

God created the sun, moon, and stars on the fourth day to decorate the stage of human activity.

"And God said, Let there be lights in the firmament of the heaven to divide the day from the night; and let them be for signs, and for seasons, and for days, and years: And let them be for lights in the firmament of the heaven to give light upon the Earth: and it was so. And God made two great lights; the greater light to rule the day, and the lesser light to rule the night: [he made] the stars also. And God set them in the firmament of the heaven to give light upon the Earth, and to rule over the day and over the night, and to divide the light from the darkness: and God saw that [it was] good. And the evening and the morning were the fourth day."(Gen.1:14-19)

They perform the role, function, and office to determine signs, seasons, days, and years for all things. And they illuminate natural light. This light defines the following names of the time: signs, seasons, days, and years.

They result from the differences in the operating cycle among the sun, moon, stars, and earth. Physically, the celestial bodies limit the operations of all things in the universe.

In particular, "signs" is a plural form of the Hebrew word

"moed" (מוֹעֵד.) Moed means a fixed time, place, and meeting. So, signs differ from seasons, days, and years. There will be selected meetings at fixed locations set by God in designated times, days, and years. The physical time by the sun and moon will determine even the religious event.

The fourth-day creation teaches that God determines the periodic operation of the celestial bodies in the universe. Thanks to this, humankind can lead a stable life on earth and measure time physically. There are four seasons out of 365 days in a year. Periodic changes in days and seasons help to know the years. The redemptive and secular history become history.

The Creation Article (Genesis 1-2) testifies that the universe and all things in it were subject to time. Science proves it. This Article said that physical time followed God's schedule. The natural world is not a coincidence but an inevitable result. Materialism or evolutionism, which explains all things by chance, is wholly rejected in the Bible.

What's like the universe subject to time? David explained it.

"Thine, O LORD, [is] the greatness, and the power, and the glory, and the victory, and the majesty: for all [that is] in the heaven and in the earth [is thine]; thine [is] the kingdom, O LORD, and thou art exalted as head above all."(1st chronicle 29:11)

Lord stands for Creator (Genesis 2:4). Naturally, all things belong to the Creator. He is the only sovereign God over the entire universe. Lord is the Highest of all. David's analogy well explains that the Lord is the Head above all.

The Head logically presupposes the body. Then, David intentionally compared the universe to the Lord's body, but Lord - to its head. He emphasized the fact that the Lord is the head of the celestial bodies.

David's body-like view of the world and the universe is the same as the biblical view of the world and the universe. The above-mentioned periodic world view logically supports it. And the Creation Article also proves it.

The plants of the third-day creation (Gen. 1:11, 12), the creatures of heaven and sea of the fifth-day creation (verse 21), and the ground creatures on the sixth-day creation (verses 24 and 25), all they came to live according to their kinds.

Thus, all things belonging to the universe are like parts of the body. They make up the celestial body of the universe. Everything, large or small, is members of the heavenly bodies. The system of the universe is like an organic structure.

All members of the body receive functions or gifts according to their role and office. And they work according to the direction of the head. The same goes well with the universe, where the Lord is the head of the celestial body. As a head, Lord distributed roles and offices among members under His plan and objective.

And under the direction of the head, the members carry out their roles. It confirms the reason why all things were created **"after their kind."** The members cannot escape from the rule of the Creator, the head. And all members, whether small or large, are essential for both the body and the head.

Here is the biblical view of the universe, the world, society, and history. Everything in the world is an inevitable outcome, not a coincidence. Even when time changes, God, the Creator, is the head of the celestial bodies forever. It is God's sovereignty, insisted by the Bible.

. **Cultural Mission**: Genesis 1:28

The cosmic creation (Genesis 1:1-25) and the cultural mission (verses 26-31) make up Genesis 1. Its structure shows that God the Creator oriented His interest from the universe toward the earth and humans. The cosmic creation was seemingly preliminary to setting up an earthly stage for the cultural mandate (Genesis1:28).

God purposely created a stage, environment, or conditions to help humanity's cultural mission. Before carrying out the cultural task, humane society always considers three worldviews: body-like, periodic, and eschatological. They provide the ideas, philosophy, and values fundamental enough to perform the cultural mission.

The cultural mission would make God's vision come true historically. For God, humankind would rule over all things on earth. His rulership would help God's Kingdom to build up in this world. Three worldviews would well guide the task to achieve God's creative purpose.

The eschatological view of the world cannot get along with the ideals, philosophy, and values to claim the world's eternity. Protology always orients itself towards eschatology. In other words, the first with a meaning of departure will achieve its purpose through the second with a sense of arrival. This worldview tells what's like the cultural mission with an eschatological consciousness.

The periodic view of the world helps discern the homogeneity and heterogeneity among the past, present, and future. It would be possible by differentiating strategic continuity from tactical discontinuity. The temporal tactics are different from one another, but they always follow the same strategy. The periodic worldview helps carry out Divine creative goals and plans transcending history and culture. It teaches how to do the cultural mandate.

And the body-like worldview asserts that the goal of creation is to construct God's present Kingdom in this world. The body is not only for itself but also for works and activities. They always are under the head of the body. The Creator, as the head of His celestial body, wants to build up and expand God's Kingdom on earth. Regretfully enough, however, works and activities for the body eventually kill itself with obesity.

The body-like worldview teaches that the present construction of God's Kingdom was the purpose of the world's existence. On the other hand, the eschatological worldview teaches that the future achievement and consummation of His Kingdom was the direction of the world's existence.

The body-like worldview asserts that the earthly world was the site to construct His Kingdom. And the periodic worldview tells that God's earthly Kingdom to be built in this world was keenly related to God's heavenly Kingdom to make its appearance in the future.

The eschatological and periodic worldviews had something to do with the consummation of the future kingdom of God. The first always reminds saints of this consummation, while the second encourages them to live in God's present Kingdom in hope for His future Kingdom. Finally, all the worldviews were subordinate to time.

What would be the human mission in this world?

"And God said, Let us make man in our image, after our likeness: and let them have dominion over the fish of the sea, and over the fowl of the air, and over the cattle, and

overall the Earth, and over every creeping thing that creepeth upon the Earth. So, God created man in his [own] image, in the image of God created he him; male and female created he them. And God blessed them, and God said unto them, Be fruitful, and multiply, and replenish the Earth, and subdue it: and have dominion over the fish of the sea, and over the fowl of the air, and over every living thing that moveth upon the Earth." (Genesis 1:26-28)

A man was God's last creation. First, God created all the conditions necessary for his survival. Then, God made him in His image. The man was like God's son, second to the Son of God. And God the Creator, as Spirit, needed a ruler over all things. God's creation of man in His image was to appoint him to rule on His behalf. All-natural elements would cooperate reasonably with humankind (Rom. 8:20-22).

Man and woman commonly shared the image of God, and the woman was equal with man. So, she had the same rulership as the man. This couple would grow, multiply, and fill the Earth. And the cooperation between them would enable the dominion over the Earth and living things of the sea, air, and ground. It is the biblical view of man and woman.

Human creation was to realize God's rule on Earth. For a while, Man's rulership was an alternative to God's dominion. Accordingly, the rulership gave the man the meaning and purpose of his existence. It is the biblical view of humankind.

However, only when God the Creator directly rules over all, God's Kingdom would go into Its consummation. It means that God would become human to materialize His dominion over human society. The Creation article already revealed that human creation presupposed the incarnation of the Creator.

However, until this completion, God's reign would be feasible with His created humans' cultural mandate. It is also the biblical view of humanity. Humankind's growth and prosperity on Earth would build and expand God's kingdom in human society.

Humanity was the only creature in the image of God. As humankind grows, multiplies, and fills the Earth, so God's rule will come true on Earth. In its turn, God's Kingdom would expand Its territory in human society every day. It is the biblical doctrine of God's Kingdom and anthropology, as well.

The cultural mandate (Genesis 1:28), aiming to build God's kingdom, was the core and conclusion of Genesis 1. The purpose of God's creation was also the same as the target of realizing God's rule on Earth. God's rule or His Kingdom, therefore, always was the constant theme of the Bible. For a while, however, man's indirect control would make it possible. It was why the Creation article (Genesis 1-2) first mentioned this theme.

The biblical worldview tells that universe is the body of God, and the Creator was its head. Common sense says that the body does not exist for itself. And the members do what its head directs. Likewise, all the universe elements work together under the Lord to construct and expand the kingdom's territory.

As time passes by, the world also changes its natural appearance and atmosphere. But the body and head still work all the time for the same purpose. The Creator, the head of the universe, always works according to God's predetermined schedule.

God achieves the strategic goal by setting different tactical targets at different times. Every tactical purpose of each era, showing the same strategic objective, repeats itself differently, and develops. Thus, many other tactical targets contribute to the strategic goal's final achievement: to build God's kingdom. Likewise, the repetition and development of biblical revelations are like the periodicity of the divine Creation.

The concept of time also governs the redemptive history of the Bible. And even humans live their own lives in different times with the change of time. Each time, they try to achieve what the cultural mandate aims (Genesis 1:28). The mandate has two divided commands: one related to humanity itself, but the other - to humanity's work.

	1st mandate	2nd mandate
receiver	Man and woman	
theme	Humanity's growth, multiplication and filling the Earth	Dominion over earthly creatures

object		Humanity/personal	Nature/impersonal
science		Human-sociology/medical	Nature science
aim	1st	Human advancement	
	2nd	Building up God's kingdom	

The first says about the growth, prosperity in human society, and the filling of the Earth. All humanity has to carry out this command. Then, all people have to love one another. The biblical Creation says that human sociology should be ethical: no love for neighbors, no cultural mission.

The second tells about the Earth's subduing and the reign of sea, land, and sky creatures. Humans from the soil depend on the earthly products for their continual survival. They have to manage nature well and distribute its products equitably. Love toward neighbors can fulfill this command well. It is the biblical view of ethics.

From a scientific perspective, the first mandate relates to the human social sciences, including human-related medicine: medical science, humanities, politics, and economics. All they need scientific growth and development. However, the second mandate relates to natural science: mathematics, physics, biology, chemicals, and geography, cosmology. These sciences study the scientific laws of the universe and nature.

The objects of their researches constitute an organic organization, another name of which is the universe. Humanity and nature are in close connection with each other. Medicine, humanities, sociology, and natural sciences are independent in studying. However, they are actually in an organic relation according to the world's biblical view and the universe.

The old scientific community had studied them individually. Then, the scientific organization fell into confusion and chaos. Lately, the community has found that all things in the world keenly link themselves with one another. By breaking down and connecting boundaries, they could solve the problem of scientific confusion and chaos.

The concept of linkage gave a new understanding that the sum of parts is much more significant. The idea of a link has become an original scientific method. However, the Creation article already mentioned that human sociology and natural sciences are an inseparable pair or couple because habitants live in the habitat.

The Creation article wrote that the universe is like God's body, and its head is the Creator. The head and body continue to work together for one purpose to construct the kingdom of God. For example, the biblical view of the world, such as the body-like universe, asserts the inseparability of God's sovereignty from the present aspect of God's kingdom.

The cosmos is God's universal realm. However, God's kingdom will build up in human society on Earth, one of the celestial bodies. It is the biblical doctrine of God's kingdom. Both the redemptive and secular histories go forward to build God's kingdom on Earth and will eventually reach the goal, showing repetition and development. It is the spiral view of history in the Bible.

The Creation article (Genesis1-2) refers to the creation of visible nature. The natural world must be in continual preservation until God reaches His creative purpose. Toward this end, the Creator planted an unchangeable law in the natural world. The universal world became a world of science and common sense. Humanity studies this world by reason.

However, the universal world was the result of God's creative plan and purpose. The will and project of the Creator, invisible Being, precede the things as seen. Faith, other than reason, is also needed. Only the grace of redemption induces people to own the belief in the Creator.

There is a difference between reason and faith. The reason is related to the natural world, but faith - to the supernatural world. As the Creator precedes the creatures, so faith is above reason. It means that reason cannot be everything. In other words, science and common sense are not omnipotent.

"Through faith we understand that the worlds were framed by the word of God, so that things which are seen were not made of things which do appear." (Hebrew11:3)

. A strategic goal of cosmic Creation

The Predestination and Election of God the Father aimed to

found God's family. Toward this aim, God the Son created the universe, nature, and humans as the Creator. Its purpose was to build God's Kingdom through human participation. Father's Decrees and Son's Creation predict that only citizens of God's Kingdom will eventually become members of God's family.

God's Kingdom requires a specific object and area. God created the universe and nature as the place of rule and humans as the rule's object. Nature and the universe will be a place of history and culture to realize God's Decrees. The cosmic creation (Genesis 1) reveals that God's strategic goal is God's Kingdom.

b.   **Earthly Creation**: Genesis 2

Genesis 1 records the universal creation, while chapter 2 - the unique creation. Like the periodicity of Creation, content repeats and develops. Repetition and development are characteristic of Hebrew literature.

This literary feature explains the content of a text more deeply and diversely. The first half and the second half of each scripture in the psalm below are a good example.

"Create in me a clean heart, O God; and renew a right spirit within me. Cast me not away from thy presence, and take not thy holy spirit from me. Restore unto me the joy of thy salvation, and uphold me [with thy] free spirit."(Psalm 51:10-12)

These verses reveal remarkable parallels. The second half repeats the first half in another way. Still, it gives more profound interpretations: 'to create in me a clean heart' and 'to renew a right spirit within me,' 'to cast me not away from thy presence' and 'to take not thy holy spirit from me,' 'to restore unto me the joy of thy salvation' and 'to uphold me [with thy] free spirit.'

Chapter 1 records the human creation and his cultural mission (Genesis 1:26-28) with God's universal creation in the background (Genesis 1:1-25). It seems to support heliocentrism. On the other hand, Chapter 2 focuses on human creation and his covenantal duty with God's earthly creation in the background. It seemingly helps geocentrism.

These chapters enrich the biblical meaning and content of God's Creation.

Genesis		Chapter 1st	Chapter 2nd
God		Omnipotent Elohim	Covenantal Jehovah
God's works		Six days	6th day
theme		God's kingdom	covenant
humanity	Man	Holder of God's image	Holder of God's life
	Male & female	Horizontal	vertical
God's kingdom		cosmic	earthly
Man's duty		Cultural mission	Creative covenant
Military terms		Strategic purpose	Tactical aims

In Chapter 1, God's kingdom (Genesis 1:26) was His unchangeable strategic purpose. From a strategic point of view, the first chapter of Genesis says about the cosmic Creation. However, the second chapter introduces it from a tactical perspective (Genesis 2:17): how to achieve God's purpose of cosmic Creation. In short, Chapter 1 reveals a strategic goal, while Chapter 2 - tactical methods.

In terms of theology, the God of Genesis 1 was the almighty God Elohim, whereas the God of Chapter 2 was Jehovah, God of the covenant. And in terms of anthropology, the man of Chapter 1 was a glorious being in God's image (Genesis 1:27). It was why he gained rulership on behalf of the Creator (Genesis 1:26-28). However, the man of Chapter 2 was a humble being out of the Earth (Genesis 2:7). Surprisingly, he signed the Covenant of Creation (Genesis 2:17) with Jehovah God.

In Chapter 1, a human was a servant of God as executor of the cultural mission. The relationship between God and man was vertical. However, in Chapter 2, Adam represented humanity and was a covenant partner equal to God. The relationship between God and man was horizontal. It is biblical theology and anthropology based on God's Creation.

In both Genesis 1 and 2, humans could exist as the result of God's Creation. However, there was some difference between them. Chapter 1 introduces humans under (or in) the unilateral grace of Creator, but Chapter 2 - in the covenantal relationship with Creator. Here are the theology and anthropology taught by the Creation article. The Creator was Christ, the Son of God before His incarnation. You may replace the Old-Testamental expression, in or with Creator, by New-Testamental phrase, In or with Christ.

Humanity should perform the cultural mandate (Gen. 1:28) by not-taking fruits from the tree of knowledge of good and evil (Gen. 2:17). Humanity's obedience will enable the kingdom of God to build up in human society. Otherwise, humankind would set up men's kingdom on earth.

Therefore, the cultural mission requires love for neighbors, while the tree of good and evil knowledge - love for the Creator. Only two kinds of love would help construct God's kingdom in human society. God is love itself, and His love is a grace of perseverance. Here are the biblical ethics and doctrine of the kingdom of God and anthropology as well.

The 2nd chapter of Genesis is not a mere repetition of the 1st one. The first tells about the strategic purpose of building up the kingdom of God. But the second introduces the tactical methods to accomplish the goal; Sabbath (verses 2:1-4), creation of human (verses 5-7), planting the Garden in Eden (verses 8-16), the law of the tree of good and evil (verse 17), systems of marriage, couple, and family (18 -Verse 25).

If you reverse their order, you will find a surprising lesson.

. **Marriage, couple and family**: Genesis 2:18-25

First of all, the practice of the cultural mission begins in the community of family. Human creation, aimed at the achievement of purpose to build God's kingdom (Genesis 1:26-27), testifies well. The man and woman of chapter 1 (v. 27) developed into a couple in chapter 2 for the institution of marriage, couple, and family (vs. 18-25). As a man and woman or as a couple, Adam and Eve began to assume the cultural mandate first in family life. It is the biblical doctrine of God's kingdom and family.

God, the Creator, didn't like Adam's aloneness and solitude Genesis 2:18). The conduction of the cultural mission made it inevitable for human society to grow, prosper, and fill the Earth. To this end, God equally formed man and woman in Chapter 1, but God created Eve with Adam's rib. Eve was Adam's helpmeet (Genesis 2:21-23). God unequally formed them in Chapter 2.

Family is the smallest unit of human society and is the smallest community, maintained by love. However, the family needs a social order. In its turn, the social hierarchy also requires inequality between men and women. Of course, man and woman equally shared the cultural mandate.

But they were inequal in having received the law of the tree of good and evil. First, God gave Adam the law, and next, Adam should teach Eve this ordinance. As the head of a family, Adam was like a king, a priest, and a prophet. However, social order is not the problem of power but love. Adam should not be an authoritarian but sacrificing leader.

The biblical concept of family was toward achieving the great goal of building God's kingdom. But the secular view is for the temporal happiness of a family. Today, the family view of the world is more popular than the family view of the Bible. Satan's strategy and tactics against the Creator seem to have won.

Adam and Eve, as a married couple, formed the first family on earth. A couple is the smallest unit of a family. The future happiness of the family relies on the level of satisfaction between them. The children, who will be born in the future, learn from them at home. Marital life between them also determines the future social life of their children. It is the biblical view of human society and family.

Sexually, couples are different. Their name implies that they have different personalities. In the family role, they are husband and wife. And in the relationship with children, they are father and mother. The first two are personally different between the couple, while the latter two are different in connection with children. However, they have a common goal of building God's Kingdom. In this respect, they are like one body (Gen. 2:24).

The couple sees diversity in the lives of their marriage,

couple, and family. The difference between Adam and Eve much more helps each other. Diversity raises the synergy between them. The variety between them is not a mistake, but a difference. Diversity and difference always focus on the effective and efficient accomplishment of one goal to build God's Kingdom. It is why variety can maintain unity.

Creation's biblical article teaches the organic relationship among individuals, families, human society, and God's kingdom. Without this link, the kingdom of God cannot build up in human society. The balance and harmony among them are essential. Democracy, which emphasizes only individual equality and freedom, or totalitarianism, which highlights only the group's interests, is not the biblical view of politics and ethics.

. Tree of the knowledge of good and evil: Genesis 2:17

Why did God plant the tree of the knowledge of good and evil at the center of Edenic Garden? Without this, the Garden of Eden would have been a perfect paradise for humanity. Without crime, there would have been no death, and Adam and Eve could have lived happily forever.

The tree played an important role in revealing the Edenic garden not as a utopia (Luke 23:43) but as the perfect paradise to come in the future. It is the biblical view of the world and utopia.

And the Creation article revealed that paradise was a gift from God. Human society's thoughts and philosophies, asserting the feasibility of constructing a utopia in this world, would be fantasy, and its efforts would always be in vain. Modern and progressive theology with the same assertion is no exception. It is the biblical view of God's kingdom and paradise.

The ordinance about good and evil was God's command. It was a symbol of authority and the law of God, the Creator. At the same time, it was the Creative covenant concluded by God with Adam (Hos 6:7). When he kept the law's covenantal condition, he could have enjoyed the covenant's promised blessing. His descendants would be no exception in it. The opposite would bring forth death to them. Thus, the law was another name for the covenant (Psalm 78:10).

Thanks to Creation's unilateral act, humankind enjoyed the unconditional grace to live in the Edenic garden. As a covenant of grace, the covenant of Creation had a different name for the covenant of obedience. Humanity should obey the law's covenantal terms so well that he could continue to live happily in this grace. Logically, however, the unconditional grace of God preceded the conditional one of the law. The cause and reason for obedience lay in both Divine graces, unilateral and bilateral. It is the biblical view of God's Law.

The tree of good and evil knowledge claims that the action of judgment on good and evil belongs to God's sovereignty. Therefore, a hasty ethical decision by men is like usurping the authority of God, the Creator. It will push them to live suffering lives day by day, eventually leading to death. Humankind, bearing the image of God, is the same brothers before the Creator. He must not allow himself to judge others in God's place. It is the biblical view of ethics.

There was a definite reason not to judge quickly. Man is a copy of God, but not the original. There would be three problems with human judgment. Humans themselves were always imperfect. Their decision would become incomplete and still relative, depending upon situations and circumstances. And people could not predict what kind of results their judgments would bring forth in the future. An assessment of good or evil would make him suffer from the hard-to-bear bridle for life.

The fruit of the knowledge of good and evil was a natural one. It did not have any magical power to help know about good and evil. Eating the fruit has two meanings: the lousy intention to usurp God's sovereignty and the betrayal of the life-giving master.
The choice would signify the will of man to become a god. And the betrayal would indicate the rejection to trust in the Creator, as in God. The fruit was God's way and means of knowing the hidden will of man in the heart.

The Creator was the only legislator and judge in the world. His judgment was righteous and just. So, God had to examine human actions as well as their motives. While genuinely loving God, humans could sometimes disobey because of their imperfection. At this time, God, having examined the heart's reasons, would judge actions (1 Sam. 16:7). God is always pleased with heartful obedience, based on the love of God and neighbor.

Only self-intentional obedience, derived from God's love, makes possible the rule by law in human society. In this way, the reign of God would come true in human society, and accordingly, the kingdom of God would build up in this world. Thus, God's purpose in creating all things in the universe would reach its goal at last. It is the biblical view of politics.

However, self-intentional disobedience, derived from self-love, means the wrong decision to usurp God's sovereignty and betrayal of the life-giving master. Human law, instead of the law of God, govern human society. The rule by human virtue will be the eventual result of atheism and nontheism, as well.

No matter how good is the government by virtue, it will result in death. The tree of good and evil knowledge teaches that the divine rule by law is the only way to eternal life. It is the biblical view of politics, governance, and leadership.

The ordinance of good and evil teaches how to carry out the cultural mission (Genesis 1:28) to build God's kingdom. Not by judging others, but by loving God, the Creator, and neighbors as brothers. It is always possible to love neighbors only when we obey God, the Creator, the lawmaker, and the judge. Both faith and love work together to build the kingdom of God.

The ordinance of good and evil is a test for human society.

This test indirectly implies the existence of Satan, who will use the fruit to tempt humankind. Before the Fall, he already existed and secretly functioned in the Garden of Eden (Genesis 3:1). Without him, humanity would not have fallen. Satan, therefore, was the cause of the sin of disobedience.

Even if Adam did not pick up good and evil fruit, the result would be the same. Satan would tempt some of Adam's descendants, and in consequence, they would eat the fruits. Regardless of Adam's Fall, one human race will divide himself into two. It was because God the Father already determined predestination and election before creating the world, and in its time, they will surely come true.

Adam had free will. Obedience or disobedience was Adam's option. However, Adam, inclusive of his descendants, had in himself the probability of disobeying God. Then, every action would come from the human will. Humanity can break at any time. But some of them will be redeemed by God, and He will make them His people. Thus, the tree was useful historically to realize the Predestination and Election of God.

After all, Satan's existence is nothing more than a method and a means to help fulfill God's Pre-creational plan. It is the biblical view of Satan, the mortal enemy of God, the Creator.

. **Garden of Eden**: Genesis 2:8-14

Before concluding the Creation covenant (Genesis 2:17), God first created Adam out of the Earth and planted a garden in Eden, his residence (Genesis 2:8-16).

The Garden of Eden was only a tiny area of the world created by God, the Creator. However, it was the center of the world. The four rivers originated from there and wet the Earth (Genesis 2:10-14). At its center were planted the tree of life and the tree of good and evil knowledge.

Then, what is the Garden of Eden?

The Garden of Eden was where religion and politics met. In Eden, God met Adam and had fellowship with him. Here, God commanded Adam to carry out a cultural mission (Genesis 1:28) and signed a creative covenant with him (Genesis 2:17). The Eden was also like the Garden of God (Ezekiel 3:19) and the palace where the Creator worked to rule.

The kingdom of God was where religion and politics became one. The Garden served as an outpost for the kingdom of God. Gradually, its territory will expand from there to the end of the world. The Garden was the starting point for this. Eden was a base for the kingdom of God.

The kingdom of God was an invisible entity. However, God ruled using the geopolitical place of Eden as a base for advancement. This location testifies that the kingdom of God already existed in the Garden. The Garden well says about the present entity of God's kingdom in the creative age.

The Garden of Eden was where God's kingdom and human society met. For the first time in human history, a family and home started in the Garden of Eden. Thus, Human society also first began with this family. From the Garden of Eden, humanity will grow, multiply, and fill the Earth.

Adam and Eve were a superior being, created in the image and likeness of God. They were God's children. As they increase in number, so does human society. Along with it, God's Kingdom will also expand further.

In the creational era, Human society and the kingdom of God were the same ones. Families were going to form a community and human society. In the Garden of Eden, all kinds of human activities began, including religion, politics, economy, society, and culture. God's rule went together with them, and accordingly, God's Kingdom would build up in human society. Human society itself would testify to the present existence of the kingdom of God.

In God's creative world could not exist the confrontational dichotomy between human society and God's kingdom, which pushes to abandon one of them. The logical dichotomy that holds both of them by logical precedence is entirely biblical. It is the biblical view of God's kingdom and the world.

The Garden of Eden was where the camp of men and the tent of God meet together. The Garden of Eden was both Adam's residence and workplace. And it was the place where God the Creator and Adam the creature met each other

(Genesis 2:8). Eden was a tent-like tabernacle of God, and at the same time, was a camp-like house of Adam's life.

In Eden, the worship of the Creator could not separate itself from the life of Adam. When the two went together, Adam's life would become a living sacrifice offered to God. Only this faith life makes it possible for Adam always to get a consciousness of standing before God. The Garden of Eden explains well what's like godly life.

The Garden of Eden was where coexisted the tree of life and the tree of good and evil knowledge. The fruit of life did not have any magic ability to produce eternal life, and the fruit of good and evil did not give any intellectual power of good and evil, either. It was just the fruit of a natural plant.

They taught that obedience not to eat the fruits of good and evil would enable Adam and Eve to enjoy eternal life. The fruit was just for testing, while the fruit of life - just a symbol, teaching that eternal life will be the price of obedience.

At the center of the Garden were co-planted two conflicting fruits. They asserted that eternal life in Eden was conditional, and the Garden was not a perfect paradise. Perfect paradise would not allow two conflicting trees to stand together. The book of Revelation well testifies to it. New Jerusalem will be an ideal paradise with only a tree of life without any tree of good and evil knowledge (Rev. 22:1-5).

The Garden of Eden was like a symbol and type, foretelling a true paradise (Matthew 25:34) and revealing a possibility to enter into there through sanctification after justification.

The Garden of Eden was where God and Satan coexisted. Satan, the enemy of the Creator, coexisted in the Garden of Eden (Genesis 3:1). Satan, using a serpent, tempted Eve, wife of Adam. God deliberately allowed his activity of temptation. Even before the Fall, there was evil in the Garden of Eden. The Garden could not be a perfect paradise. It means that Satan's existence in charge of evil was also inevitable for the holy Creator.

Theologically, the Creation record asserts monism that the Creator is the only God. It is a never-changing truth. However, God's intentional permission gave Satan to act in this world. Historically or phenomenologically, dualism looks like truth.

There are two kinds of dualism. Cosmological dualism argues that the good and evil gods with equal power in hands fight against each other forever in the universe. It is dualism from a religious point of view. And metaphysical dualism argues that both the spirit and flesh equally quarrel with each other in a person. It is dualism from an ethical point of view.

Human history testifies to the constant struggle between good and evil. Dualism supports this circular or cyclical view of world history. At one time, evil prevails, but finally, good wins. And at another time, just defeats unjust, but unjust overcome again. But the good and just is always the final winner.

However, the Creation article denies dualism. Satan and evil are temporarily allowed by God. In the universe and the world, the Creator is the only omnipotent God. There can be no other gods. They are nothing but idols. God is so almighty that He could achieve the purpose of His creation. He involves and controls everything from start to end and also between them.

The Garden of Eden was the first paradise for humanity. The Creation article of the Bible also speaks of utopia. However, a utopia or paradise is God's creation, not humans' one. It means that humankind will never establish a paradise in the world with their wisdom and power. Someday in the future, the utopia will come down from Heaven as God's gift for humanity (Rev. 21:1-2).

If Eden were a real paradise for humankind, God would not have commanded Adam to build His kingdom on Earth. Instead, God wanted to test humanity so that He might select the people who will enter the real paradise, God's Kingdom.

The divine Predestination and Election already divided humanity into two groups: in Christ and out of Christ. This division will historically come true by testing them. Only humankind, striving to obey God and establish the divine realm in this world, will become the citizens of God's real kingdom. The Garden of Eden explains well the biblical doctrine of God's Kingdom and Soteriology.

The two aspects of the Edenic garden give us the biblical view of the world. This world was favorable to the Creator in that God would make it His divine realm sooner or later. However, God's present kingdom would be just a symbol and type of God's future one. The prototype will eventually appear when the earthly type disappears. In this respect, this world was unfavorable to the Creator.

The biblical worldview is double-folded: optimistic and pessimistic. Humankind has to make double efforts: to get along with the world on the one hand and to go far away from it on the other hand. The dual attitudes toward the world are a pearl of biblical wisdom for faith life.

"But this I say, brethren, the time [is] short: it remaineth, that both they that have wives be as though they had none. And they that weep, as though they wept not; and they that rejoice, as though they rejoiced not; and they that buy, as though they possessed not. And they that use this world, as not abusing [it]: for the fashion of this world passeth away."(1st Corinth7:29-31)

. **Created Man**: Genesis 2: 7

God's Kingdom is the kingdom where God Himself rules. But God delivered His rulership to His created man. When humans rise to the level of God, the kingdom of God will reach complete consummation. It will be possible only when God Himself becomes human. Until this time, God needs a human co-worker. It is the biblical doctrine of the Divine Kingdom and anthropology.

"And the LORD God formed man [of] the dust of the ground, and breathed into his nostrils the breath of life, and man became a living soul." (Genesis2:7)

The Creator formed humans out of the dust, and He breathed the breath of life into the nose. The breath of life is another name for the spirit in the Bible (Job 32: 8, 33: 4). The human out of soil became a man, as a living soul. Man is a soul, possessing a spirit. The presence of the spirit enabled the appearance of personality and animal life in the human body. When the spirit leaves, they also disappear from man accordingly.

Therefore, man is composed of spirit, mind, animal life, and matter. Man is a four-dimensional being: spiritual, psychological, intuitive, and material. In other words, man is a religious, social, animal, and economic existence. Man is an organic being, compositive of four dimensions.

It is impossible to know a person by one of them. It is a piece of too partial knowledge. The good examples are communism with emphasis on material and psychology with a basis on sexual instincts. Anthropology, emphasizing only the religious aspect, is not an exception.

Of course, the spirit is the most fundamental for man. The spirit, however, reveals himself through the mind and body. And humans, working for the construction of God's Kingdom, are in constant relationship with the Creator, nature, and human society. The study on four dimensions makes it possible to know humans holistically.

And the anthropology of dichotomy or trichotomy derives

from Greek dualistic philosophy. It comes from a phenomenological point of view, rather than creationism. Each of them asserts the opposite relationship between the spirit and the body. They always conflict with each other. The upper layers of spirit and mind represent religious and social dispositions, but the lower layers of animal life and material are animal intuition and economic essence.

Humanity frequently suffers the internal conflicts between spirit and matter or between mind and instinct. In nature, the spirit is heavenly, while animal instincts and economic needs are earthly. Man, himself, is a paradoxical or contradictory being, standing between heaven and Earth.

These conflicts develop themselves into the spiritual battles between the kingdom of God and the kingdom of men. Besides this, they become an ideological war between the ways of thinking by time and by space. Humanity always feels this existential conflict. It is the biblical doctrine of anthropology.

Genesis 1 refers to humans from the perspective of God's dominion, while Genesis 2 - from the point of anthropological existence. At this point, Genesis 2 is not a mere repetition of Chapter 1. The Creation Article (Genesis 1-2) teaches fundamental doctrines: Theology, anthropology, soteriology, and God's Kingdom.

. **System of Sabbath:** Genesis2:1-3

The Creation article recorded the Sabbath system

immediately after the cosmic creation. The seventh day after 6-day creation (Genesis 1) was Sabbath (Genesis 2:1-3). God declared that Sabbath was holy and blessed.

The Sabbath was a day dedicated to God and distinguished from the other six days. According to the Sabbath system, human society must work hard for six days and rest on the 7th day. A weekly system appeared.

The Sabbath system also supports the spiral view of history in the Bible. The time and days physically and periodically repeat and keep moving forward. However, as the Sabbath, the seventh day was one of the 'moeds' described like signs. Human beings created should gather home and worship God the Creator at every feast of the Sabbath.

After the 6-day creation, the Sabbath was the first rest to God. It was the same with Adam. Created human first rested. Then, he began to work on the first day of the week. First, relax and later, do! It was natural. God had already prepared everything for the created man.

After resting on the 7th day of Sabbath, he only had to act and work in Eden's Garden. Work after rest. The Sabbath rest gave him the strength to work for six days. It was the way how created humans first began to live his life.

Having rest on Sabbath, he could meditate on the Creator and, at the same time, reaffirm the purpose and meaning of his existence from the creative perspective. And he worked. In this way, he could readjust the direction and goal of his life. Thus, the creative Sabbath helps people fundamentally think about their existence and experience.

Sabbath rest means not only cessation of work but liberation from work. Cessation and liberation. This cessation liberates people from the physical and mental burden of work. Freedom has a double effect. It helps them look back on what they did yesterday and, at the same time, creatively approach what you plan to do tomorrow. Thus, the Sabbath rest after work was so important.

The work for six days makes humanity stand as a practical being, while the rest of the Sabbath – as a religious and speculative being. Sabbath rest so helps that he could reflect on life religiously and philosophically. At this time, humanity could reaffirm that the visible space and the material world were not everything. He readjusts his experience with the way of thinking by time, but not by space. Sabbath also helps men to become spiritually alive. Physical rest becomes a spiritual one.

On the contrary, the lack of Sabbath rest buries human society in works and actions. Thus, it will forget or lose the meaning and goal of existence and life, supported by the Divine Creation. And it would become a slave to work. However, human society has to learn the meaning of psychological and religious rest through a physical one. It is so necessary to know and understand the balance between work and rest.

The Sabbath also has a sociological meaning. The Sabbath

system was a law commanded by God, the Creator. On Sabbath, all men, young and old, poor and rich, were liberated from all kinds of works. There was no difference between master and slave in this respect. Moreover, livestock had to rest.

No one could stand against this right. The Sabbath system itself asserted equal rights among people and advocates social equality. This system reconfirms that all created human beings are equal before God, the Creator.

And the Sabbath system also has a theological meaning. The Creator rested on the 7th day after having worked for six days. Rest after work. The six-day Creation symbolically foretells that God will continue to work toward the purpose of God's creation (John 5:17). But at the moment of achieving the creative goal, God will no longer work and rest forever (Hebrews 4:10).

Then, humankind will also have eternal rest (Matthew 25:34). So, the creative Sabbath is the type and symbol of this eternal Sabbath. The Sabbath system also revealed that there would be a time when God will fully consummate the creative purpose.

The Creator did not work without any aim and plan. The Sabbath system revealed that when God's kingdom builds up in a perfect sense, humans will also meet the eschatological Sabbath. The Sabbath system also pushes people to think about all things by way of time, but not space. The spiral view of history in the Bible explains well what view of the world and life the Bible supports.

. **Tactical targets of earthy Creation**

The five items examined above are God's tactical methods (Genesis 2) to construct God's Kingdom on earth (Genesis 1). In reverse order, it is even more apparent.

The Sabbath system already foretells an eschatological rest and that God's Kingdom will be a kingdom of freedom and equality.

Human creation reveals that human participation will make it possible to build God's Kingdom. Ultimately, it tells the incarnation of Christ, the Son of God.

Eden's founding means that God's Kingdom will start small, but its glory will cover the whole world in the future. The ordinance of good and evil tells that God's Kingdom will be governed by the rule of God's law, not by human virtues.

And the systems of marriage, couple, and family indicate that the construction of God's kingdom begins with a couple and expands with a family.

c. **God's creative world**

The Creation article publicly announced that God had begun to work by His creative action. The beginning already foresaw its ending, as well as the process between them. God was the Creator, Ruler, and Finisher. God, as the Sovereign of all things, had to be the head of them.

"For of him, and through him, and to him, [are] all things: to whom [be] glory for ever. Amen." (Rome11:36)

The Divine ministry of creation made two different things like a couple: nature and supernatural, science and theology, reason and faith. Only the belief in God's creation helps people to interpret all things in harmony by a logical dichotomy rather than a confrontational dichotomy.

However, the Creation belief denial pushes people to choose dualism and live life by a biased and closed way of thinking. The good examples are the ideas, philosophy, and values supporting atheism. It's because the denial leads to thinking by reason on the phenomenon world. Without the fear of Jehovah, the Creator, they lose the beginning and foundation of knowledge and wisdom (Proverbs1:7).

God's strategy of Genesis 1 was going to accomplish its purpose with God's tactics of Chapter 2. Even though human history and culture change diversely, the tactical meanings or principles of Chapter 2 cannot alter. Their teachings are still valid today as Christian thoughts, philosophy, and values.

God's created world comprises cosmic creation (Genesis 1) and terrestrial creation (Genesis 2). Both the outcomes had the same purpose of realizing heavenly reign or establishing God's Kingdom on Earth. The former provides the stage of God's Kingdom, while the latter introduces humans as its citizens.

That's why the cosmic creation emphasizes the cultural mission (Genesis 1:28), while the earthly one - the creative covenant (Genesis 2:17).

Broadly, God's created world was the combination of the following worlds: universe, nature, animal world, and human society. As the head, the Creator supervises all of them for the earthly realization of God's reign. The Creator keeps them under His power. In God's cosmic and terrestrial world, the happenings, small or large, cannot escape from the rule of the Creator.

The Bible records numerous kinds of narratives. The Creator God (A) is the Master and the King. His will and providence govern nature (B), human society (C), and individual saints (D). God, nature, humane society, and individuals, comprising one body, maintain an organic relationship.

It is theoretically possible to study each of them individually, but it is historically impossible for them to be independent. Research's theoretical results should organically link themselves together. Then, the results show harmony and balance in interpretation.

The Bible is like a narrative story made jointly by God, nature, society, and individual man. It is possible to divide the biblical narrative mainly into four types:

God-centered: AB, AC, AD (3 kinds)
Nature-centered: BA, BC, BD (3 kinds)

Society-oriented:　CA, CB, CD (3 kinds)

Individual-centered: DA, DB, DC (3 types)

The first combinations show that God works directly. However, the second to the fourth show that God works indirectly through nature, human society, and individuals at different times. Every narrative of the Bible belongs to one of these combinations.

Focus on God means the influence of theology on natural science, social science, and individuals. Emphasis on nature says about the impact of natural science on theology, social science, and individuals. Accent on humane society tells about the influence of social science on theology, natural science, and individuals. The individual's accentuation testifies to the impact of personal character on theology, natural science, and Social Science.

Contrary to Greek dualism, Christian theology does not separate itself from natural science and humane sociology. The above combinations claim that the life of faith is holistic. And they explain in detail what's like the life of faith. The narrative varieties can help the saints live a life of faith strategically and tactically.

Even as time passes by, the Creator remains forever as the head of the creative world. The world also continues to exist until the time to consummate the purpose of Divine creation. It is why God created the sun, moon, and stars in the universe.

They periodically designate signs, years, seasons, and days. The creative world, therefore, is subordinated to time, but not space.

Cosmic creation was a preliminary step for terrestrial design. In other words, the background of the terrestrial world was the cosmic creation controlled by time. Humans have to remind that keeping God's creation covenant and doing human's cultural mission are also time-limited ministries.

The Bible always supports both the eschatological and spiral view of history, redemptive or secular, until its end. After all, creation faith is a philosophical belief in the world and history subordinate to time. The teachings of Genesis 1 and 2 always remain valid until the end of the Bible. It must be the beginning, basis, and principle of biblical ideas, philosophy, and values.

2.   **Fall:** Genesis 3

Adam was the only ancestor of humanity. He was like a seed with countless numbers of identical ones. Human society already existed in himself. As a representative, he signed the Creation Covenant with God, the Creator, by the tree of good and evil knowledge (Genesis 2:17). In him, humanity also joined this Covenant. The future of his descendants would depend on the obedience of Adam.

The first man, Adam, was a type of Jesus Christ, the second and last Adam to come (Rom. 5:12-21). It is Christology from the anthropological perspective. However, anthropology also contains Christology in itself. On the other hand, Christ, the Son of God, will fulfill and complete the Father's Decrees. The Creator had to be the Pre-incarnational Christ. It is also Christology from the theological perspective.

There was no problem with the latter's Christology, but with the former Christology. The first man, Adam, was not a complete copy of Christ. And God, the Creator, already planted the fruit of good and evil knowledge at the center of Edenic Garden. God commanded him not to eat from the tree (Genesis 2:17). However, he was likely to disobey.

Unfortunately, Satan, the mortal enemy of God, already existed in the Garden of Eden (Genesis 3:1). God allowed Satan to test Adam. Holy God could not directly tempt him to lead to death (James 1:13). For a while, Satan takes control of sin, injustice, and death instead of Holy God (Ephesians 6:12). However, as one of God's creatures, Satan is always under God's sovereignty, the Creator (Job 1:11, 12, Luke 22:31).

a.   **The origin of evil**: Genesis 3:1

Before the Fall, Adam and Eve lived happily in Paradise Eden. Then, however, Satan, the archenemy of God, already existed there. Satan acted under the guise of a serpent (Genesis 3:1-7) even before the Fall. There was an apparent possibility of evil with followings: tree of good and evil knowledge, Satan, and his activities.

Why and for what did God allow this?

The Creator was the only God, and then Satan was his creation. The Creator permitted Satan, His adversary, to work in Eden. It means that his existence would, in some way, serve the Divine creative purpose (Genesis 1:26-28). God's allowance has a positive meaning.

And God, as Father of all, is ontologically loving. Even His love granted satanic existence and his evil activity. It was undoubted that the tolerance would indeed contribute to the achievement of the purpose of Divine Creation.

The fruit of good and evil knowledge played a role in the testing method, while Satan – in the tempting part. The examination or temptation presupposes passing or dropping. It would divide humanity into two groups among Adam's descendants. And Adam himself had a potential possibility to give birth to winners or losers in temptation. Whether or not he loved his Creator would decide the winner or loser in Satan's temptations.

Was God, as the Creator, the author of sin? If there weren't both Satan's existence and the tree of good and evil, Eden would have been a perfect paradise. Conversely, Eden testified itself not as a real paradise. The Garden of Eden was a test site. There Adam would not forcedly but voluntarily choose whether he will obey or not. For this test, the Creator gave Adam a full sense of free will.

Adam, created in the image of God, should not betray his Creator by himself. So, there must have been a tempter. God, the Creator, allowed Satan to play a tempting role. The Bible also seemingly supports dualism. The Creator, however, is only one God, and Satan is one of His creatures. The Bible fundamentally insists on monism.

Dualism is more attractive than monism because humans have a strong tendency to see only phenomenal appearance. However, as the Head of all, God well controls even satanic existence and his evil activities. Satan is just a servant of God.

Otherwise, it would be impossible for God to achieve His purpose and plan, set before the foundation of this world. Satan and evil act and work only temporarily in this world until God achieves the goal of His Creation. They are always under the sovereignty of God.

Human society, therefore, cannot eliminate evil artificially or intentionally. And satanic existence argues that humankind cannot establish a paradise or utopia in the world with their wisdom and power. It is the biblical view of Satan and Paradise. Christian church and theology should pay keen attention to these biblical teachings.

In the Garden of Eden, Satan, not revealing himself, indirectly approached Eve in the outer appearance of a serpent (Gen. 3). It is the way how Satan and injustice always work in human society. They, using a medium, ever seduce people. It is a Satanic strategy and tactics. Apostle Paul explains this well.

"And you [hath he quickened], who were dead in trespasses and sins. Wherein in time past ye walked according to the course of this world, according to the prince of the power of the air, the spirit that now worketh in the children of disobedience. Among whom also we all had our conversation in times past in the lusts of our flesh, fulfilling the desires of the flesh and of the mind; and were by nature the children of wrath, even as others." (Ephes 2:1-3)

Nevertheless, Satan cannot work at his will. The book of Job testifies well to it (Job 1:12, 2:6). Of course, social events and evil phenomena in human society are the results of Satanic activities. At the same time, it is the result of Divine acceptance. Looking at the events and phenomena, a godly believer also looks for God's will behind them. He is not in a hurry to criticize or judge the social evils and injustices carelessly or prematurely.

Satan continues cunningly to tempt human society and the church. He skillfully tests it in the form of ideas, philosophy, and values. They assert that without God, the Creator, or Redeemer, humanity can live happily. God, allowing these satanic activities, selects between grains and tares. It is why devout saints do not hurry to evaluate them from a philosophical or political perspective.

This moment, the godly never forgets that Jesus should love even enemies (Matthew 5:44). He understands that even the sins and injustices of the world work for God's will. Jesus, therefore, advises us to repay evil with good, not evil (Luke 6:35).

His advice has some effects. Saints try to abstain from all appearances of evil (1 Thessalonians 5:22). They can play a role as salt and light to break the corruptive cycle with good. And unbelievers, seeing their deeds, praise and glorify God, the Creator. It is the Divine will toward the saints living in this world.

When human society denies God, the Creator, he is likely to judge by what appears. It is why he always fails in every temptation. However, believers should be the winner.

"**The righteous will live only by faith.**" Saints already enjoy the grace of redemption by faith. After salvation, they have redemptive faith as a new way of thinking and do not judge by reason alone what they see.

They have a regenerated reason, obtained by faith in the Creator and Redeemer. The faith always urges them to know and trust God the Creator as the Master of all. Only this faith enables them to see behind social evil and injustice in the world. Church history proves this very well.

World history also tells that many nations and peoples, rising and falling, appeared and disappeared on earth. But the church still exists in this world. It is a surprising result of overcoming evil with good or of subduing reason with faith.

b. **The event of Fall**: Genesis 3:2-7

The tree of good and evil knowledge did not have any

magical power to know good and evil. Its fruit was a symbol of the authority of God, the Creator. Not following the rules means disobedience to the Head of God, the Creator. Obedience, however, would be an act of faith in the Creator, as in the Master of all.

The obedience of observation was another name of the faith, and they cannot separate themselves from each other. The observance is a faithful confession of striving to realize Divine rule in human society, as God wants. This confession helps humankind think out the ideas, philosophy, and values based on the concept of time, not space. And it urges them to search the Divine plan and will beyond all social events, too.

However, disobedience is an atheistic confession that humans, denying Creator's Lordship, want to become a master in His place. From then on, what humanity see by sight becomes everything to him.

Rejecting God's rule of law, he tries to build up a dominion by his virtue. To this end, he has to redefine his existence, life, the world, and history from an atheistic perspective. Human thoughts, philosophy, and values become secular and mundane.

The ordinance of good and evil has conditions and promises. Based on this ordinance, a covenant between God and Adam was equally concluded (Genesis 2:17, Hos 6:7). It was God's unconditional grace. This statute of good and evil first became God's most simple law, as another name for the covenant.

God's unconditional grace demanded His conditional grace from Adam as representative. Keeping the law means keeping the covenant. God promised to bless or curse Adam on these covenantal conditions. Therefore, Adam had a full sense of freedom. It is the biblical doctrine of covenant and law by the Creation article.

Keeping the covenant or law by humankind will realize God's rule in the Garden of Eden. The more humanity prospers, the better God's Kingdom builds itself and more broadly expands in human society. The realm of His dominion will spread from Eden until the end of the world. Naturally, human society will be happy under His power. It is the doctrine of the kingdom of God by the Creation record.

However, by breaking the covenant, the human would get the lordship instead of the Creator. From then on, he, being an incompetent ruler, would carry a heavy yoke to judge good and evil upon neighbors. Poor judgments would cause him and his neighbor to suffer psychologically and physically, leading to death. It would be the unfortunate result of a broken relationship with the Creator of Life.

The life outside the covenant meant life outside God's Kingdom. In other words, those out of God's covenant had to be out of the Garden of Eden. And also, it was like being outside of Christ, the Creator, even before His incarnation. Only the curse of death would await them. There would remain such a wholistic curse on fallen humanity.

Immediately after the Fall, God did not judge humankind to

death. God had not yet achieved the purpose of His Creation. Moreover, among the fallen humanity, there would remain a group, chosen in Christ before the creation of the world. Until their redemption, God should still show mercy, goodness, and lovingkindness upon the fallen humankind. It is God's common grace upon them.

God's common grace helps the fallen humankind set up a social order even in a corrupted society. Therefore, it would also apparently show supreme goodness and beauty in ideology, philosophy, and values. Reason and common sense of fallen humanity help maintain the order. But it was fundamentally under sin and death. Regretfully enough, humanity could not redeem itself.

God directly gave Adam the commandment to keep the ordinance of good and evil (Genesis 2:17). Satan, knowing this well, could tempt not Adam but Eve. She learned this statute from Adam. And Eve was bone of his bones and flesh of his flesh. So, Satan tempted Eve, knowing that Eve could be Adam's weakness.

Eve, having been enticed by Satan, could easily defeat Adam. Then the first family would collapse, and thus, Adam and Eve could not carry out the cultural mission. This way, God, the Creator, could suffer failure in the purpose of God's Creation.

"Now the serpent was more subtle than any beast of the field which the LORD God had made. And he said unto the woman, Yea, hath God said, Ye shall not eat of every tree of the Garden? And the woman said unto the serpent, We may

eat of the fruit of the trees of the Garden: But of the fruit of the tree which [is] in the midst of the Garden, God hath said, Ye shall not eat of it, neither shall ye touch it, lest ye die."(Genesis3:1-3)

God commanded not to eat only the fruit of good and evil knowledge. However, the snake provocatively said whether God told her not to eat all of Eden's fruits and intentionally stimulated Eve to stand against God psychologically or emotionally. Having heard him, Eve glanced at the fruit of good and evil amid the Garden. It looked better than the other fruits.

Then, Eve should have remembered Adam, who had said to her that God forbade eating. Instead, some complaints and doubts arose in her mind. Satan's sudden provocation shook Eve's mind. She answered, saying that God forbade not only to eat but also to touch the fruit, lest she dies.

Eve thought that God had forbidden even to touch and sensibly feel the fruit. It was evidence of hidden complaints. And Eve vaguely replied, **"If you eat the fruit of good and evil, you might die.**" This expression seemed to be a kind of doubt. Using this chance, Satan again tempted her to ignite dissatisfaction with God's command and distrust coming from her subjective perspective.

What was Eve's fault? Eve did not understand that the core of His law was God's love for Adam and Eve. Instead, she perceived it from an ascetic perspective. At this moment, she forgot that humans, as the subject of faith, should believe as commanded by God, as the object of faith. God's word was more important than her subjective perception and emotion.

The negative perception led her emotionally to avoid the words of God. At that time, she, instead of the psychological avoidance, should have faced what God said and meditated upon it carefully.

True love toward God, the Creator, would have helped firmly believe in the merciful purpose of God's law. In its turn, her heart would have become warm with God's love. Faith would have come from the head down to her heart. Thus, faith and love would have helped her positively understand God's ordinance of good and evil. On the contrary, Eve viewed God and His law too negatively.

"And the serpent said unto the woman, Ye shall not surely die. For God doth know that in the day ye eat thereof, then your eyes shall be opened, and ye shall be as gods, knowing good and evil." (Gnesis3:4-5)

The serpent's temptation revealed impure aims. The serpent persuaded Eve, saying that she would not die even if she eats. He turned God's words into lies. Furthermore, he asserted that her eyes would brighten when she eats, and she would know good and evil like God. The serpent cunningly recommended an idol-worship instead of the God-worship. Humanism also claims that man can become God.

In this test, God was invisible, but serpent the tempter - visible in her sight. And God tested her by His word. However,

Satan tempted her by visible things that appeal to the five senses. Eve had to choose God's word or serpent-distorting lie. People prefer what is visible to what is invisible. And they more like to listen to complaints to soothe themselves.

"And when the woman saw that the tree [was] good for food, and that it [was] pleasant to the eyes, and a tree to be desired to make [one] wise, she took of the fruit thereof, and did eat, and gave also unto her husband with her; and he did eat."(Genesis3:6)

The fruits looked good for food, pleasant to the eyes, and desirable to make her wise. They appealed to Eve more than the words of invisible God. Besides this, the promise of God's word belonged to the future. It was less appealing to her.

On the other hand, she could feel the visible fruits in her hands. People always prefer visual space to the invisible time, which they cannot sense as real entities. Satan knows man's limitations and weaknesses.

Eve picked up the forbidden fruit of good and evil knowledge. Then he invited Adam to eat together. Adam unhesitatingly ate some part of the fruit. Didn't Adam know the result at this moment? He surely knew. To his regret, Adam could not refuse Eve.

Eve was the flesh of his flesh and bone of his bones. Adam and Eve were like one body, indivisible into two. Adam could not leave Eve alone in a state of curse. As the head of his family,

Adam, feeling responsibility, willingly chose the covenantal curse together with Her.

Adam's arbitrary disobedience prophesied that Christ, as a second Adam, will not leave the church, as His bride, under the curse (John 3:29; 2Cor.11:2; Ephes.5:25-27). Christ also will voluntarily carry the sin of His bride (Hebrews 2:13-18). Thus, Adam, the first man, was the Messiah's type to come (Rom. 5:14) and the symbol of the second and last Adam (1 Corinthians 15:45, 47). It is Christology by Creation and Fall article (Genesis1-3).

Adam and Eve sinned against God, the Creator, by having eaten the fruit of good and evil. The first disobedience became an original sin to cause death as its price. All humankind did not commit the same sin, but they are now under the same curse as Adam (Romans 5:12-14). Humanity inherits original sin from generation to generation. The created man became a fallen man. A fallen man will become the re-created man only when he becomes a redeemed man.

God's test method always has two aspects: religious(theological) and social(ethical). The test leads us to decide whether or not we love the Creator as well as our neighbor. The trespass of having eaten the fruit of good and evil denied God's authority and, in its turn, destroyed both the love for God and neighbor in the end. Creation articles do not separate theology and ethics or faith and love. Both of them are like both sides of a coin.

The disbelief and disobedience toward the Creator make humanity a master of life. People put all their hope in the visible world. They fight one another for more possessions. And they are ready to judge neighbors with the help of good or evil. Love for neighbors breaks down in that society. Sooner or later, human society becomes a world where the law of the jungle and the fittest survival are famous.

The ordinance of good and evil was the same test method used by God and Satan. However, the results are entirely different, depending on who is the tester. Divine test targets the spiritual growth of saints, while Satan's temptation aims at the spiritual ruin. God is good, just, and right forever, while Satan – deceiver.

Another difference lies in that God promises future blessings by words, while Satan tempts people by visible things. Which one are people willing to choose bitter test or sweet temptation? The painful test leads to eternal life, while the sweet temptation – eternal death. Most fail in this test.

In a word, Fall means denying God, the Creator, and choosing Satan as the new master. Having obeyed Satan, Adam handed over to him the rulership upon all things. Satan, as a new ruler, began to dominate humanity. Naturally, people will suffer from his lordship and, in the end, will meet eternal death. Fallen humankind needs a Redeemer.

c.   **Protoevangelium**: Genesis 3:8-24

Disobedience forced Adam to sell himself to Satan as well as his rulership over the world (Rom. 6:16). He was outside the covenant, that is, out of the Creator, Christ before incarnation. Adam was under the power of sin and death. Satan became the new master.

As a natural being, the fallen humans cannot free himself from Satan's power as a supernatural being. The Creator had not yet achieved the purpose of His Creation. Above all, He had to redeem the fallen humanity. Immediately after the Fall, He promised a Redeemer (Savior).

"And I will put enmity between thee and the woman, and between thy seed and her seed; it shall bruise thy head, and thou shalt bruise his heel." (Genesis3:15)

The first promise and prophecy of the Redeemer are called Protoevangelium. It was a real beginning and basis of all the promises, revelations, and predictions about the Coming Messiah. The Creator, cursing the serpent, declared to him the promise of redemption. It meant that His future Redemption would result in Satan's destruction.

Without the snake's existence, there would have been no temptation to seduce Eve to sin. The destruction of the serpent meant that he would make humanity tempted no longer. In other words, his defeat would imply the salvation of fallen humankind. It is why the Protoevangelium is also called the Redemption Covenant.

Who would be the Savior, revealed in the original Gospel? He will be the woman's seed to break the snake's head, while the serpent hurts the heel of the woman's seed. The head injury will be fatal, but the heel injury - not so deadly. The fight between them will be so decisive that on the one hand, the woman's seed could enjoy a final victory, and on the other hand, the snake should suffer a lethal defeat.

A woman's seed meant a descendant born out of a woman. However, the serpent was a beast, instigated and exploited by Satan. So, the snake represented Satan. At the same time, a descendant from the woman is a natural being, while Satan - a supernatural being. To win this fight, the descendant out of the woman must be mightier than Satan. God alone is stronger than Satan.

Therefore, the original Gospel predicted the Creator's future incarnation, the Son of God, as the Father's Decrees (Ephesians 1:3-6) revealed before the foundation of the world. Only when the Creator, as the Spirit, becomes a Man, the Divine Predestination and Election will be entirely fulfilled and consummated.

The Protoevangelium foretells the decisive battle between the woman's seed and the serpent and other types of fights: between the woman and the snake, and between the woman's seed and the serpent's seed.

In the first fight, the relationship between Eve and the snake was inherently intimate. This intimacy was the leading cause of the Fall. God had to break their keen relationship and made them enemies of each other. That's why people hate snakes, and they alert people.

Here was hidden a surprising prophecy. Adam, Eve and the serpent symbolically represented Christ, the church as His bride, and Satan (Revelation 12:9, 20:2). Accordingly, the battle between woman and serpent was like the spiritual war between Christ's church and Satan. Satan, as the new lord of the world, would always persecute the church. The church unilaterally suffers. Church history testifies very well.

The next fight would take place between the woman's seed and the serpent's seed. The original Gospel already predicted that one human would come split into two kinds of spiritual groups. The snake's seed means the descendants belonging to Satan, but the woman's seed – the descendants belonging to Christ's church. Spiritually, they would work for either Satan or the church. They would continuously fight each other.

In all the fields of ideas, philosophy, and values, human society comes split into two religious groups: theistic or atheistic. Spiritual battles happen between the Church and Satan, and also between their members. In these struggles, the churches and believers, alienated from the world, are always under one-sided suffering and persecution. Jesus told his disciples about its cause.

"If ye were of the world, the world would love his own: but because ye are not of the world, but I have chosen you out of the world, therefore the world hateth you. Remember the word that I said unto you, The servant is not greater than

his Lord. If they have persecuted me, they will also persecute you; if they have kept my saying, they will keep yours also. But all these things will they do unto you for my name's sake, because they know not him that sent me." (John15:19-21)

There can be no compromise between them. It is because the world does not know the Heavenly Father and Christ, His Son (1John 3:1). The world has no choice but to hate the church and its members. Therefore, He prayed to the Father for His disciples' spiritual safety, who would remain in the world after His Ascension.

"And now I am no more in the world, but these are in the world, and I come to thee. Holy Father, keep through thine own name those whom thou hast given me, that they may be one, as we [are]." (John17:11)

"I pray not that thou shouldest take them out of the world, but that thou shouldest keep them from the evil." (John17:15)

Spiritually, saints cannot belong to this world. And they cannot stand as neutrality between Christ and Satan. They fight with the Gospel in these battles. The Gospel proclaims that Jesus Christ, the dead and risen, is only Lord of hosts. Satan, boasting himself as master of this world, always persecutes His disciples.

The former two fights will end in the third fight between the woman's seed and the serpent. This fight will be completely different from the former battles. The former conflicts are indirect proxy wars, but the third battle will be a direct all-out war between Christ and Satan. This fight will separate the Old Testament from the New Testament. Only Christ will bring victory to the church and the saints.

Why was the Messiah compared to the "**seed**"? The biological function of the seed theologically explains Christology and Soteriology very well. Although the seed is one, it has many identical ones inside it. In this meaning, the seed is singular and, at the same time, plural. The woman's seed will be a special one. The seed is like a representative. He will fight directly with Satan for the plural grains latent in the seed. His victory will be their victory (John 12:24).

Like this, the original Gospel (Genesis 3:15) prophesied that the Creator, Christ, would be incarnated as the Redeemer. Before the incarnation, Christ, as Creator, ruled, and controlled human history. After the embodiment, He will fight and win Satan. After that, he will ascend and sit at God's right hand as the new Master of the world and anew rule human society. Jesus's resurrection and ascension have this theological meaning.

When the Son destroys Satan by His death, He will also fulfill humanity's redemption and salvation. But their consummation will be possible when He throws Satan into the lake of fire forever. Until this time, the first and second battles will continue in this world with guaranteed victory on the saints' side.

Churches and believers need not despair amid suffering and persecution. Christ's Second Coming will put Satan in the lake of fire forever. Satan will no longer be able to tempt humankind. Then the redeemed saints will get into the stage of glorification where they can no longer sin. God's Kingdom will finally reach its consummation.

The single seed of the woman will give triumph and victory to the multiple ones of the woman. When will it be possible? His advent has something to do with the time of God's achievement of the creative purpose. His Coming also has a close relationship with the fulfillment of redemption promised in the Protoevangelium. Even His coming for the promised redemption cannot escape from the concept of the Divine time emphasized by Creation because the promised Redemption will be an eschatological one.

Thus, the Protoevangelium was the covenant of Redemption that looked forward to the fulfillment and consummation of saints' redemption by Christ, the Son of God. Even after the Fall, the covenant helped Adam and Eve live the nomadic life of faith, overcoming the desperate life out of the Garden of Eden.

d. **Result of the Fall**: Genesis 3:7-19

The action of obedience was the very confession of faith in God's Creator. The obedient are allowed to live under the grace of God. They, enjoying God's grace on earth, shall eventually reach the promised eternal life.

But the act of disobedience was a clear confession to disbelieve in the Creator's Mastership. The disobedient live their lives outside the grace of God and will ultimately get to eternal death.

What was the curse that Adam and Eve experienced every day after the Fall?

. **Personality division**: Genesis 3:7

Shortly after having eaten the fruit of good and evil, Adam and Eve knew that all they were naked. Immediately they became ashamed of each other. Previously, they praised each other's beauty by looking at the same nakedness. And they thanked God for it.

After the Fall, however, the opposite happened. In a hurry, they covered their shame by making skirts out of fig leaves. Before and after the Fall, they always saw the same objects. After the Fall, however, they began to recognize each other differently. The beauty of God's creation turned into shame. Why was it?

The act of disobedience was an expression of the will to reject God and judge good and evil by oneself. It immediately cut off the relationship with God, the Creator, and darkened Adam's spiritual eyes. This darkness gave a negative influence and change to the world of their perception.

The sin of disobedience distorted the spiritual realm of men and the world of their perception. Because the matter of praise turned into a matter of shame, and Adam and Eve looked at each other negatively. There happened a problem with their personality and thinking. As one body, they were already unhappy. The sin of not-keeping God's covenant was fatal to their character.

. Spiritual division: Genesis 3:8

One day Adam and Eve heard the voice of God walking in the Edenic Garden. Their reactions were much different from before. They, feeling ashamed, hid behind a tree to avoid the face of God. They were like Children, unwillingly avoiding beloved Father. It was so unnatural.

God called Adam, saying, "**Where are you**?" This question was not about his locality but his spiritual condition. In the past, Adam would have come to God happily and quickly. At this moment, however, Adam hid in fear of God.

Adam replied, saying, "**I am afraid and hid behind a tree**." Soon God asked if Adam had eaten the fruit of good and evil knowledge. At this time, Adam should have immediately confessed and repented his sin. Instead, he showed the hardness and stubbornness of his heart.

"And the man said, The woman whom thou gavest [to be] with me, she gave me of the tree, and I did eat."(Genesis3:12)

He blamed God and Eve for his trespass. Sinners do not know how to repent by themselves (Psalm 51:10). Sin spiritually separates God and Adam. As a result, Adam was already under Satan's hand. The sinner cannot free himself from Satan. Likewise, sinners drive themselves away from God, the Master of life. It was spiritual death as a curse brought by spiritual division with God.

. Social division: Genesis 3:12

The spiritual division by sin causes not only personal division but also social division. Adam said that the cause of evil lay in Eve. Before the Fall, Adam referred to Eve as the flesh of his flesh and bone of his bones. After the Fall, however, he hated Eve. In those days, the first family was society itself. Sin split the social relationship between the couple.

And when God asked Eve for sin, she showed the same unwillingness to repent as Adam. She also blamed the serpent for the cause of sin. Her violation was rooted in willful determination. Therefore, forgiveness would be possible only by confessing and repenting the heart's evil before God. However, a sinner under Satan's bonds cannot repent by himself.

Adam and Eve's accusations testify that sin makes a person's heart harder and harder than ever. Their allegations were an excellent testimony to how severe was the level of hardness of their heart.

Human character is the seat of intelligence, feeling, and will. Even if Satan tempts him to sin, he cannot sin without willful determination. Humans must take responsibility for their actions.

It is neither God nor Satan but the man himself that makes sin.

. **Division of marital life** (Genesis 3:16)

Next to Eve, God blamed the snake for the sin. The cause of the evil lay in the snake. God foretold his destruction and declared the Protoevangelium (Genesis 3:15). And next, God cursed Eve.

"Unto the woman he said, I will greatly multiply thy sorrow and thy conception; in sorrow thou shalt bring forth children; and thy desire [shall be] to thy husband, and he shall rule over thee."(Gensis3:16)

God's curse will make Eve's life more suffering. The woman will give birth in pain and much more long for her husband than ever. Nevertheless, the husband will rule over his wife more strongly than ever. Before the Fall, childbirth was blessings to God and humankind. After the Fall, however, it turned into pain. They would be able to taste the joy after a painful birth.

Eve first fell into temptation. To avoid repeating future mistakes, Eve would love her husband more, and Adam was likely to have more control over his wife than ever. This kind of couple life would add another suffering unto the wife. So, male-priority and female-slaves to husbands became an ordinary and universal custom in world cultures.

. **Collision with nature**: Genesis 3:17-23

Adam also received a curse by God.

"And unto Adam he said, Because thou hast hearkened unto the voice of thy wife, and hast eaten of the tree, of which I commanded thee, saying, Thou shalt not eat of it: cursed [is] the ground for thy sake; in sorrow shalt thou eat [of] it all the days of thy life. Thorns also and thistles shall it bring forth to thee; and thou shalt eat the herb of the field; In the sweat of thy face shalt thou eat bread, till thou return unto the ground; for out of it wast thou taken: for dust thou [art], and unto dust shalt thou return." (Genesis3:17-19)

God condemned Adam for the cause of the Fall. He, as the representative of humanity, made a covenant of Creation with God. Adam, on behalf of the Creator, became the ruler over all things. But he failed in keeping the covenant with God. It was because he listened not to God, the Creator but his wife.

Adam's disobedience made the world condemned. God's curse was more severe and broader. It was through life's hard work that Adam could barely feed his family. Before the Fall, farming was pleasant labor for fulfilling the cultural mission, while, after the Fall, agriculture - a painful one.

As a result of God's condemnation, thorns and thistles came out of the ground. They much hardened labor of farming and also drastically reduced harvests. People out of the soil had to rely on what came from the land. Accordingly, they consciously or unconsciously depend on visible space more than ever. Eventually, the spatial way of thinking dominates the fallen humanity more strongly than ever.

Originally, Adam was born of dust. His origin was truly lowly. However, he was second to God, the Creator. To regret, the sin of disobedience brought him back to humble soil. Thus, fallen humans would live an unhappy life on earth and eventually return to dirt.

. **Parting with the Garden of Eden**: Genesis 3:22-24

"And the LORD God said, Behold, the man is become as one of us, to know good and evil: and now, lest he put forth his hand, and take also of the tree of life, and eat, and live for ever. Therefore the LORD God sent him forth from the Garden of Eden, to till the ground from whence he was taken. So he drove out the man; and he placed at the east of the Garden of Eden Cherubims, and a flaming sword which turned every way, to keep the way of the tree of life."(Genesis3:22-24)

The judgment on good and evil was the fundamental responsibility of the Creator. After the Fall, however, Adam came to know good and evil like God and would behave himself as a judge upon good and evil. If fallen humans further ate the fruit of life, they would become equal to God, and accordingly, the purpose of Creation would be impossible to achieve.

First, God drove them out of the Garden of Eden. Next, He took measures to make it impossible for them to approach and eat the Tree of Life. God's condemnation pushed humanity to cultivate the land to which he belonged. The agricultural life outside Eden was outside God's covenant and, that is, life without Christ.

Farming in the Garden of Eden was fun. Agriculture had helped carry out the cultural mission. And it would help advance to the next level humanity out of the earth. After the Fall, nature would not help humankind well. Farming outside Edenic Garden would be painful.

God's curse was to make humanity cultivate the land from which God had taken him. The Fall resulted in missing the opportunity for a man of the dirt to become a man of heaven. He came back to the earth. The soil became his only hope. He had to survive by relying on what belonged to the ground more than ever.

The soil or land was the only source of power and wealth in agricultural life. Accordingly, people belonging to the earth, naturally or unconsciously, lived life on a spatial way of thinking rather than a temporal way of thinking. Eventually, spatial thinking would dominate the fallen humanity. It would prevent them from seeing and hoping for Heaven.

After the Fall, nature would no longer help humanity. He had to conquer nature for survival. Nature conquest indirectly symbolized conquering the deity who created it. In agricultural societies and cultures, humans finally become gods and absolutes. After the Fall, farming life and culture lead humankind forcedly to live a cursed life.

The Fall took away the opportunity for him to belong to heaven forever. Instead, he came back to the dirt again. From the human sociological perspective, the biblical Fall well explains what kind of life fallen humanity will live after the Fall, and what result will await him.

e.   **God's mercy and compassion**: Genesis 3:21

"Unto Adam also and to his wife did the LORD God make coats of skins, and clothed them.   And the LORD God said, Behold, the man is become as one of us, to know good and evil: and now, lest he put forth his hand, and take also of the tree of life, and eat, and live forever: Therefore the LORD God sent him forth from the garden of Eden, to till the ground from whence he was taken." (Gensis3:21-23)

God showed His mercy and compassion upon Adam and Eve before their expulsion from Eden. First, God made leather coats and clothed them. Then, He sent them out of Eden to plow the land. Adam and Eve changed the skirts out of fig leaves into the leather coats made by God.

Unlike the fig skirts, the leather coats almost permanently covered their shame. For this, God had to kill beasts. Only redemptive death made it possible to hide their shamefulness. The leather garments recalled them to remember the redemption promised in Protoevangelium (Genesis 3:15).

Redemption would be possible only through the ransom. Like the ransom with the beast's death, the woman's seed will die for the atonement of fallen humankind. It was God's grace and mercy upon the fallen and lost amid judgment of wrath (Lam. 3:22).

Protoevangelium and the leather coats were like Gospel for Adam and Eve, who had to live in despair outside Eden.

f.   Two cultures at war (1)

The Creation Article (Genesis 1-2) tells that the world and humankind made their first appearance by God's creative action. The first man had a mission to realize God's rule in an eschatological world.

On the contrary, the Fall Article (Genesis 3) writes about Adam and Eve, who failed the test due to Satan's temptation, God's enemy. They, not obeying God, the Creator, rejected God's creative purpose.

The first battle occurred between God and Satan and ended with Satan's victory. However, Protoevangelium (Genesis 3:15) revealed that God the Creator would seek the fallen to stand again before God by His redemption.

The Fall destroyed Adam's spiritual relationship with God, the Creator. It meant the loss of life and the acquisition of death, as well. Thus, Adam and Eve returned to the soil, out of which they came. Agriculture would become the only way of living on earth.

3.   **Flood Period**: Genesis 4-9

Since Genesis 4, Primeval History had continued with the following theological themes on a background: Creation (Genesis 1-2), Fall (Gen 3), and Redemption (Gen 3:15).

Humanity becomes divided into two groups as already foretold in the original Gospel: The godly who believe in Creation and Redemption and the ungodly who oppose them. Naturally, there always remain two groups showing the difference in thought, philosophy, and values.

	Creation	**Fall**	**Redemption**
anthropology	God's children	Satan's slave	Reborn children
habitat	In Eden	Out of Eden	
faith	Creationism	hedonism	Creationism
thinking	Temporal way	Spatial way	Temporal way
rule	Christ	human	Christ
philosophy	Creationism	evolutionism	Creationism
culture	farming		shepherding

From the Fall to the Flood, Primeval History records four events: the first murdering, the ancient human civilization, Enoch's ascension, and the mixed-marriage.

a.   **Cain and Abel**: Genesis 4:1-15

Before the Fall, Adam and Eve were physically healthy. After the Fall, they very much wanted to get the seed promised in the Protoevangelium (Genesis 3:15). Adam knew Eve, and she conceived. Eve gave birth to Cain and Abel (Genesis 4:1-2). It meant that they lived not so long enough in the Garden of Eden and rushed to fall.

The names - Cain and Abel - expressed their parents' state of mind after the Fall. Cain means hope in despair, but Abel - the distress due to the Fall. In other words, Cain's significance was finally to acquire the "woman's seed" prophesied in the original Gospel (Genesis 3:15), while Abel's meaning - "vain" after the Fall.

Adam and Eve firsthand witnessed the Creation (Genesis 1-2) and Fall (Genesis 3). In contrast, Cain and Abel, as the first generations not participating in the two epochal events directly, experienced all their results. How would they live their lives in a whole new era?

According to the natural order of birth, Parents thought that Cain, the eldest son, was a woman's seed. However, the original Gospel could not follow the natural rank. The seed of natural birth would not hurt the serpent representing Satan (Rev. 20:1-3). The seed would have to be more potent and mightier than Satan (Matthew 12:29). Christ, the Son of God, must become a descendant of a woman.

Therefore, Adam's descendants by blood and flesh would

not be qualified to become a woman's seed. Woman's seed, as Coming Messiah, would not have to inherit Adam's original sin. The Son would come from a woman who would not know a man (Isaiah 7:14). At that time, Adam and Eve did not realize this theological meaning. However, they firmly believed in the original Gospel and eagerly waited for the Messiah.

Both Cain and Abel were of Adam's bloody lineage. Growing up, Cain and Abel became a farmer and a shepherd, respectively. Thus, the Bible naturally records agricultural life and nomadic life together.

Anthropologists argue that a long time passed until agricultural life settled in human society. They also say that human culture had developed as follows: gathering life, hunting life, nomadic life, and farming life.

However, the Bible ignores these prolonged periods and simply records both lives simultaneously. There were theological and sociological reasons for this. Cain and Abel, as a grown-up, had to confess for the first time what kind of faith in God they had.

The Protoevangelium (Genesis 3:15) had already foretold that one human would split into two. Their confession revealed to what they would spiritually belong. Faith and act of obedience are like two sides of a coin. As the action is evidence of faith, so it is another name for faith.

Cain offered the fruit of the ground to God, while Abel - the firstlings of his flocks and its fat. God accepted Abel and the offering but did not accept Cain and his offering. At this time,

Cain, the eldest son, was very angry with his younger brother, and his face fell.

The original Gospel (Gen. 3:15) already promised the Redeemer. And before driving Adam and Eve out of Eden, God also revealed to them how God would redeem them. Having killed the beast, God made a leather coat and masked their shame with it (Genesis 3:21).

At this time, God might have killed a sheep. Lamb's ransom death would make it possible to cover their shame. Cain and Abel heard the narratives of God's Creation and humane Fall so many times from childhood.

How did Cain and Abel react to the same revelation and prophecy?

Their ways of offerings gave the testimony to it (Hebrews 11:4). Cain, the eldest son, did not believe in God's Creation and the promised Redemption. And he, ignoring the eschatological way of thinking by time, relied on the hedonic practice of thinking by space. The present visible reality was more important than the invisible God and His past Creation narrative.

He had given himself to farming. He made many efforts to get a lot of ground products. He eagerly offered to God products from grounds. But his offering was the direct products out of the cursed soils. The thorns and thistles were the symbols and unfortunate result of God's curse. Cain always had to work harder and harder for the harvest. Therefore, Cain's harvests symbolized his brilliant merits, who could finally overcome God's curse. He boasted himself before God, the Creator, by his offering.

On the other hand, Abel was a shepherd. He had tried to acquaint himself well with the biblical narratives of Creation and Fall. Abel had a firm belief and strong hope for the promised Redemption of the original Gospel. He knew well that he was living in the eschatological world. Taking into consideration the future Redemption, Abel thought that shepherding was more important than farming. He offered the firstling of the sheep and its fat. To do this, Abel had to bleed upon cursed soil by killing the lamb.

It was why he did not offer products out of the cursed land. He sacrificed as offerings the lamb that ate the products from the cursed land. The curse moved onto the lamb instead. Having shed the blood of the slaughtered sheep, Abel sacrificed it to God. Thus, the lamb died on behalf of Abel, the sinner.

By faith, Abel was redeemed and justified for the first time in human history. He knew very well that unredeemed sinners were unclean before God. Only the redeemed would be able to come before God. It was why grain offerings always followed burnt offerings (Lev. 15:3-10, Numbers 15:3-16).

It is possible to explain the difference in the ritual method between Cain and Abel from human-sociology. Creation and Redemption narratives' indifference implies the ignorance of belief in the Creator and the Redeemer to come. The present visible reality is all things for such humans. This way, people, being subconsciously dominated by spatial thinking, begin to live and work for themselves. Accordingly, the farming way of life makes people more obsessed with space, that is, land.

Many lands help to get more surplus agricultural products, and they bring greater power and authority. People come worship wealth. The ruler always has to occupy more land to expand his power and wealth. The strong exploit the weak for himself. The agricultural culture makes it harder to practice love for neighbors.

On the other hand, nomadic culture does not adhere to the land, unlike agrarian culture. From time to time, shepherds wander around in search of grass to feed the sheep and goats. They are more sensitive to the change in changeable time than unchangeable space. By missing the time to gain fodder, they meet unfortunate to lose all herds.

Nomadic society commonly shares the land for its everyday survival. Thus, nomadic life always pushes the time concept to dominate the mentality of shepherds. People can enjoy freedom and equality in a nomadic society more than in an agricultural one. The nomadic life fits the biblical principle of God's Creation and Redemption better than the agricultural one.

Later Cain secretly killed Abel, his younger brother, in the field. It was the first murder in human history. The murder reveals that false worshipers will always persecute true worshipers in the future, and two cultures will always be against each other. Naturally, two kinds of worship and culture will also fight each other in ideas, philosophies, and values, as foretold in the Protoevangelium.

Even before the murder, God had already warned Cain (Genesis 4:5).

"And the LORD said unto Cain, Why art thou wroth? And why is thy countenance fallen? If thou doest well, shalt thou not be accepted? And if thou doest not well, sin lieth at the door. And unto thee [shall be] his desire, and thou shalt rule over him." (Genesis4:6-7)

Cain did not look at himself and refused to repent. He was angrier with his brother's true faith than with his disbelief. Even today, the wicked do not see their evil doings and are more upset with the righteous's good doings. Cain was no different from Adam, his father. Adam also attributed the Fall to God and Eve rather than to himself (Genesis 3:12).

Cain's stubbornness and resentment were apparent evidence that he inherited Adam's original sin. And the wicked were unable to repent for themselves because they were evil. The outward act also reflects the inward state of mind as it is.

"The good man out of the good treasure of his heart produces good, and the evil man out of his evil treasure produces evil; for out of the abundance of the heart his mouth speaks." (Luke6:45)

The good and evil, mentioned by God to Cain, were not only ethical but also religious. Moral goodness was possible under a normal relationship with the Creator. In other words, evil is the result of an abnormal relationship with Satan. The Bible teaches that religion cannot separate itself from ethics.

The faith in the Creator makes saints' ordinary life subordinate to time, not to space. It enables them to build ethical good in heart. They produce the goodness of the heart by works. Only then can they practice both love for God and neighbors.

However, God's ignorance leads people to live their lives subordinate to space and become more and more selfish. This way of living keeps building evil in their hearts. They produce the evil out of the spirits, which manifests itself by works.

Disregarding the Creator's warning, Cain kept the evil hidden in his heart. Sin was always ready to fall at the door of his heart and, at last, took the opportunity to murder his brother Abel (Matthew 12:34-35).

God ever sees not the outward act but the inward state of mind as the cause for it. Adam's original sin became the root of Cain's homicide. Moral evil and injustice will prevail in human society, which ignores the faith in Creation and Redemption. Cain did not know that God, the Creator, was always the lawgiver, the administrator, and the judge. Naturally, he, as the master of his life, did what he wanted. Cain believed that no one knew of the secret murder he had committed. But God said to him.

"Then the LORD said to Cain, "Where is Abel, your brother?" He said, "I do not know; am I my brother's keeper? And the LORD said, "What have you done? The voice of your brother's blood is crying to me from the ground." (Genesis4:9-10)

All visible things become the most important to atheists. Nobody can prevent them from doing what they want. The more deeply they become obsessed with space concept, the more easily and quickly they do evil. It is because atheism enhances the level of corruption in human society.

Cain was sure that his murder was a complete crime. Cain was such an atheist. When God directly pointed out his murder, he could not excuse himself anymore. God judged him.

"And now you are cursed from the ground, which has opened its mouth to receive your brother's blood from your hand. When you till the ground, it shall no longer yield to you its strength; you shall be a fugitive and a wanderer on the earth."(Genesis4:11-12)

Cain's murder made the earth further cursed than ever. His life became more cursed. Even if he sweated his work, he could not deserve the price. In search of good land, he used to wander from one place to another. When he found good ground, he was ready to hurt his neighbors to take it. Human society would become more and more desolate.

Contrary to Adam's expectations, Abel, not Cain, was the woman's seed. Later he found that Cain killed Abel. Cain was of the serpent, but Abel was of the woman. Having learned about it, Adam and Eve again fell into despair. They lived as strangers in misery for over 100 years until they gave birth to Seth instead of Abel.

b. **Cain and Seth**: Genesis 4-6 chapters

When God pointed out and judged sin, Cain suffered from his heart and said:

"And Cain said unto the Lord, My punishment [is] greater than I can bear. Behold, thou hast driven me out this day from the face of the earth; and from thy face shall I be hidden; and I shall be a fugitive and a vagabond in the earth; and it shall come to pass, [that] every one that findeth me shall slay me. And the LORD said unto him, Therefore whosoever slayeth Cain, vengeance shall be taken on him sevenfold. And the LORD set a mark upon Cain, lest any finding him should kill him." (Genesis4:13-15)

There are several essential lessons in Cain's confession.

Cain was spiritually under Satan's power. In this state, he, feeling remorse, could not repent by and for himself but felt.

Cain needed God's mercy of atonement to free himself from the guilt but lacked Divine grace. Cain also knew that he could not see God's face any longer. God's curse forced him not to live in His grace. The curse made Cain a fugitive on the earth.

Under Satan's spiritual power, sinners could not enjoy rest because their psychological anxiety accompanies insecurity in life. For a while, people lived a life of gathering and hunting. Cain, a murderer, had to be always anxious that someone could murder him someday in the future.

Cain could not take part in God's special grace of redemption but still participate in God's common grace of Creation. As long as he lived, his life would always be safe (Genesis 4:13-15). Even after the Fall, human society would be in good maintenance until Divine achievement of Creation purpose.

Cain was very conscious of people other than himself. It means that there were other people besides biblical persons: Adam, Eve, Cain, and Abel. Adam gained Seth at the age of 130 (Genesis 4:25, 5:3). During this period, many other people were born out of Adam. Cain, Abel, and Seth were just written in the Bible by God's choice for redemptive history.

Cain, who killed Abel, his younger brother, could not meet his parents. To the land of Nod, east of Eden, he fled (Genesis 4:16). Thus, he left the face of Jehovah. His running away completely excluded him from the redemptive grace promised in the original Gospel (Genesis 3:15).

Cain continued to live the life of a farmer. God's curse made him work harder than ever, but the earth did not produce harvest as much as he wanted (Genesis 4:12). Cain had to wander around in search of land. In this process of survival, he had to deal with other badly. So, he used to live his life in fear of being killed by others (Genesis 4:14).

After a considerable time, Cain obtained Enoch. Surprisingly enough, Enoch from Cain was the same name as Enoch from Seth as the fifth-generation (Genesis 5:21-24). Seth's Enoch had walked with God for 300 years and ascended to heaven without experiencing bodily death. Having heard this, Cain might have named his son Enoch. Cain's family could not fall behind Seth's family. In front of the people, Cain had to hide the sense of inferiority of his unorthodoxy.

For about 700 years from Adam until Enoch's ascension, Cain had wandered from one place to another. After the birth of Enoch, however, he could build a city and named it after the name of his son, Enoch. A city of that time was a castle. Society began to settle in a castle after a long period of collecting or hunting life.

At last, the first agricultural culture had emerged in human history. Agriculture demanded settlement, and, in its turn, the settlement required building a village. The Cain family developed the architecture to set up castles. The agricultural technology and architecture ended the wandering life as a fugitive.

The castle building was inevitable to keep in safety Cain's family and his surplus agricultural products. And Lamech, Cain's fifth-generation, was the same name as Lamech, Seth's seventh-generation. It means that About 300 years passed from Seth's Enoch to Lamech (Genesis 4:17-19). During one thousand years until the Flood, Cain's descendants had mainly developed human civilization one by one: farming, architecture, herding, music, and bronze tools.

Jabal was born out of Ada, the first wife of Lamech from Cain. He became the first herder of cattle (Genesis 4:20), but not shepherd. Jubal, Yabal's younger brother, was the first musical artist (verse 21). On the other hand, Zillas, Enoch's second wife, gave birth to Tubalcain. He was the ancestor of the bronze culture (v. 22).

The members of the Cain family used Bronze utensils for farming and living. Agriculture also developed dramatically. The harvest of agricultural products was much bigger than using stones and wood as equipment.

And they could keep the surplus agricultural products safely in the city. The descendants of Cain were able to live their lives reliably, abundantly, and happily. Moreover, the bronze instrument became a better weapon to give political power to rule over other peoples.

Cain's descendants, who did not believe in God, the Creator had found an ancient agricultural civilization. People lived on the way of thinking by space, not by time. It was the result of the Fall (Gen 3). Humanity no longer believed in the Divine Creation

(Genesis 1-2) and not hoped for the future Redemption of the original Gospel (Genesis 3:15). People enjoyed only the present life of this visible world.

There arose severe problems with their civilization and culture.

"And Lamech said unto his wives, Adah and Zillah, Hear my voice; ye wives of Lamech, hearken unto my speech: for I have slain a man to my wounding, and a young man to my hurt. If Cain shall be avenged sevenfold, truly Lamech seventy and sevenfold." (Genesis4:23-24)

In the civilization of Lamech from Cain stood out bigamy, but not monogamy taught by Divine Creation. Lamech, with power and wealth, had a concubine other than his first wife.

The Creation Article (Genesis 1-2) taught that God's kingdom had to build up first in the family. However, the biblical institution of marriage, couple, and family became an instrument of physical pleasure. The family system's collapse caused human society to break down and urged God's kingdom to disrupt.

And Cain's civilization and culture were violent and cruel. Better agricultural development enabled more accumulation of material wealth and a higher possibility of possessing bronze weapons. The strong man ruled the weak with them. It was why Lamech retaliated for his small wounds with murder.

Cain's family first established a society where the law of the jungle and survival of the fittest was very famous. The better human civilization progressed and developed, the more often people killed and murdered their neighbors.

Lamech of the Cain family showed off his brutality and ferocity in front of women. It was vulgar heroism that likes to demonstrate wealth and power. Such a society was very far from the goal of God's Creation (Genesis1:26). Cain's civilization showed the typical character of an agricultural community, ignoring Creation beliefs.

About a thousand years later, after Enoch's birth, the Flood occurred worldwide. During this period, Enoch from the Cain family built a city and found a settled agricultural society, and afterward, humanity continued to deteriorate morally and ethically.

When Lamech, the fifth-generation of Cain, lived his life, the social deterioration reached the climax. Cain's community showed well what kind of future ending awaits humanity relying on the spatial way of thinking and living.

Adam and Eve, who lived a thousand years, could not give birth to only Cain and Abel. God chose them for the Divine history of redemption. Many other children were born from Adam and Eve (Genesis 5:4). And their descendants also gave birth to numerous offsprings. One hundred thirty years later, after the Fall, Seth was born to Adam instead of Abel.

In those days, the descendants of Adam, Cain, and Seth

respectively composed human society. The genealogy of Genesis 4 belongs to Cain's family line, while the genealogy of chapter 5 - Seth's family line. However, Genesis 6 records that Adam, Cain, and Seth's descendants split into two groups: God's sons and men's daughters. The sons of God represented believers in God, the Creator, while the daughters of men – unbelievers.

Before the Flood, the descendants of the Cain family found an ancient human civilization. They set up a settled agricultural society. On the contrary, the descendants of the Seth family had no contribution to the development of culture. They, still wandering from one place to another, lived a nomadic life. In those days, they were in social alienation from Cain's society. Other descendants of Adam would have also lived as the weak there.

There had been a spiritual revival for about 700 years from Enos, the first son of Seth, until Enoch's ascension. However, during the 400 years after the ascension, a spiritual decline began gradually. It had been very rapid for almost a thousand years until the Flood after building Lamech's castle. This decline eventually caused the Flood judgment (Genesis 6).

The Bible records that when Seth gave birth to Enos, people began to call upon the name of the Lord (Genesis 4:26). The spiritual revival had lasted for 700 years until Enoch's ascension. During these years, Adam's other descendants spiritually joined Seth's descendants. They became the sons of God. They also abandoned the comfortable life in the castle and lived life as nomads like Seth's descendants.

However, after Enoch's ascension, other descendants of Adam and Seth, meeting a spiritual decline, had begun to join Cain's comfortable life in the city for nearly a thousand years. They also started to live life on the spatial way of thinking. Naturally, evil and injustice were rampant in the world.

Then, who were the sons of God and the daughters of men? God's sons were those godly people who believed in the promise of the original Gospel (Gen. 3:15) and lived with hope for future Redemption. But the daughters of men were contrasted with the men of God, as godly believers. They were the daughters born out of the unbelievers who had nothing to do with the original Gospel's promise.

In other words, the godly people spiritually belonged to the woman's seed revealed in the original Gospel, while the ungodly people − to the serpent's seed. Unfortunately, The sons of God saw the beauty of men's daughters and took them as wives. The daughters adorned themselves in pursuit of pleasure. They were more beautiful than the women of the godly people who lived roughly in the mountains and fields.

Spiritually and socially, the mixed marriage between the sons of God and the daughters of men was dangerous. The marriage meant the interrelationship between the different families in religion and culture. The family believing in the Creator and Redeemer, could not get along with the family, denying this belief. Apostle Paul pointed out its spiritual danger.

"Be ye not unequally yoked together with unbelievers: for what fellowship hath righteousness with unrighteousness? And what communion hath light with darkness. And what concord hath Christ with Belial? or what part hath he that believeth with an infidel? And what agreement hath the temple of God with idols? for ye are the temple of the living God; as God hath said, I will dwell in them, and walk in [them]; and I will be their God, and they shall be my people."(2Corinth6:14-16)

Paul describes the marriage between believers and unbelievers as between righteousness and lawlessness, between light and darkness, between God's temple and idols, and between Christ and Belial.

It is possible to explain sociologically. The mixed marriage is like an incompatible pair between thinkings by time and space from the creative perspective. And theologically speaking, biblical eschatology cannot stand together with unbiblical materialism forever. It is like a contradiction between theism and atheism. Mixed marriage is like syncretism, resulting from succumbing to lawlessness, darkness, idols, and Belial.

The mixed marriage had reduced the number of devout believers in the original Gospel (Genesis 3:15). The reduction had lasted for not less than a thousand years. God's Spirit could no longer be with people (Genesis 6:3). God decided to carry out Divine judgment upon them. Then, God withdrew His common grace from them by stopping His Spirit to strive with men (Genesis6:3).

The marriage between them caused ancient warriors to appear and fight for supremacy with the Nephilim of that time (Genesis6:4). For what was the fight? Clans and tribes sought to capture more lands that would give them more military strength, political power, and economic wealth.

From ancient times, the economy has been the root cause of wars and fights. Thus, evil and injustice prevailed more and more in human society (Genesis 6:5-6). The more fundamental reason lay in the way of thinking, governed by the concept of space. As long as human culture and civilization mainly rely on the spatial territory, it is inevitable to fight one another for survival on earth.

These fights and conflicts would make it impossible to achieve the purpose of God's creation (1 Tim. 2:1-4). It is why the way of thinking by space is Satan's important ideological strategy and tactic against God. God was so grieved and lamented (verse 7).

There's a difference between the two genealogies. The genealogy of Genesis 4 records that Cain and his descendants significantly contributed to human civilization's development and progress. But they were the hedonists enjoying temporal pleasures. Shortly speaking, they lost the meaning of their existence before God, the Creator.

On the other hand, the genealogy of Genesis Chapter 5

says that Seth and his descendants had nothing to do with ancient civilization's development rather than Cain's descendants. However, unlike Cain's genealogy, Seth's one records the time of birth, death, and survival in detail. In this respect, Seth's descendants were especially beloved by God as His sons. In contrast, Cain's descendants, the founder of a splendid ancient civilization, were introduced as beasts by a single expression, 'begotten.' God's point of view was entirely different from that of man.

Seth's genealogy shows that his descendants belonged to the lineage of the Messiah to come, but Cain's genealogy testifies that his descendants were exclusive of the line. In other words, these genealogies show the following difference: the devout life in the concept of time, sincerely hoping for the grace of Redemption, and the ungodly life in the idea of space, enjoying only the present pleasure and comfort.

This difference made another tremendous result. Enoch, one of Seth's descendants, ascended to heaven without physical death. And also, they lived in reverence. They could escape from the old world and enter into a new world at the time of Divine judgment by the Flood. However, Cain's descendants lived life like fat beasts and abruptly disappeared in the Flood.

The contrast between the two genealogies sociologically explains the difference between Cain's settled agricultural society and Seth's non-settled nomadic society. In short, the distinction and difference are the ideological comparisons between the ways of thinking by space and by time. This comparison teaches a godly believer how to live a life of faith in this world.

c. **Genealogy of Seth**: Genesis 5

Seth's genealogy (Genesis 5) between Cain's genealogy (Genesis 4) and the Flood (Genesis 6-8) has a crucial redemptive meaning. It showed that Noah inherited the Messiah's pedigree lineage promised in the original Gospel. Seth's descendants played an essential role in redemptive history.

And Seth's genealogy was also culturally significant. Cain's descendants founded the ancient human civilization. They could dominate the world thanks to their agricultural life. However, Seth's descendants lived a nomadic life. Compared to the descendants of Cain, they were unknown. But they were godly, living by faith in the Divine Creation and Redemption.

. **The witness of the Protoevangelium** (Genesis3:15)

When Adam was 130 years old, God gave him Seth instead of Abel, who was killed by Cain (Gen. 4:25, 5:3). The lineage of the woman's seed succeeded again. It was as if dead Abel became alive through Seth. God did it to achieve both the Divine purposes of Creation (Genesis 1:26-28) and Redemption (Genesis 3:15).

Adam believed in the promise of the original Gospel more firmly than ever. Adam, Eve, and Seth eagerly preached the first Gospel to people. At the age of 105, when Adam was 235 years old, Seth gave birth to Enos. From then on, people began to call on the name of Jehovah (Genesis 4:26). At least 200 years passed after God expelled him from the Garden of Eden.

Since then, the revival of faith had continued for about 350 years. The revival met the culmination by the event of Enoch's ascension. More than 700 years had passed since the birth of Seth. Until Methuselah, Adam's 7th generation, people enjoyed a long life close to one thousand years.

All ages from Adam to Lamech, Noah's father, had survived and known Enoch's ascension. The ascension greatly encouraged Seth's descendants, who fervently and diligently believe in the original Gospel. The Epistle to Hebrews said:

"By faith Enoch was translated that he should not see death; and was not found, because God had translated him: for before his translation he had this testimony, that he pleased God. But without faith [it is] impossible to please [him]: for he that cometh to God must believe that he is, and [that] he is a rewarder of them that diligently seek him.."(Hew.11:5-6)

The names of Seth's genealogy testify competently to the fever of the spiritual revival. Enos, Seth's son, means a weak human being. Humans have their origin in the dirt (Genesis 2:7) and are inferior beings who must return to soil due to the Fall

(Genesis 3:19). Thus, Seth confessed that they had to believe and hope for the Messiah to come, promised in the Protoevangelium.

Cainan, Enos's son, means getting in the same meaning as Cain. It implies that Enos eagerly awaited the seed of the woman, promised in the original Gospel. Mahalaleel, Cainan's son, means praising God. It was a confession of faith that he praised God, who showed favor and grace to Seth's sons, living as strangers in this world.

Jared, Mahalaleel's son, meaning seed, well expressed the faith and hope for the woman's seed, promised in the original Gospel. Enoch, Jared's son, representing the dedicated, contains Jared's earnest wish for his son to live a life entirely dedicated to God. Enoch ascended unto Heaven without physical death.

Enoch's ascension event provoked two repercussions in human society. Seth's descendants held on to the faith and hope of the original Gospel more firmly. However, it was a shame for the descendants of Cain, the ruler of ancient human society. The ascension damaged their pride. Cain's descendants, the founder of ancient human civilization and culture, could not allow their glory and names to fall any longer.

They began to use names similar to those of Seth's descendants. Enoch, Seth's sixth generation, was the same name as Cain's second generation, and Lamech, Seth's eighth generation, had the same name as Cain's fifth generation. Furthermore, Cain's descendants from the 3rd to 4th generation had similar words to Seth's sons from the 4th to 7th generation.

After Enoch's ascension, the heat of faith became more and more relaxed, and nearly 700 years later occurred a flood to destroy the world. There remained fewer and fewer Witnesses who lived a heavenly life. About 250 years before the Flood, the patriarchs from Adam to Enoch, the sixth generation, did not live any longer, and only Methuselah, Lamech, and Noah survived.

For about 1,700 years before the Flood, both Cain and Seth's descendants had been fruitful and multiplied. For almost 800 years in the first half, Seth's generations had believed and hoped for the promise of the original Gospel, living a life that was distinct from Cain's ones. However, for about 800 years in the second half, the men of God, including Seth's sons, gradually abandoning the promise, married the daughters of men, mainly descendants of Cain, and became secularized. The spiritual decline was more severe during the 250 years before the Flood judgment (Genesis 6: 1-2).

Genesis 4-5 records the flow of redemptive history amid secular history after Adam's Fall. Seth's sons, insisting on Creation and Redemption's faith, lived an ascetic nomadic life, while Cain's sons, denying this faith, lived the pleasure-seeking agricultural life. Thus, Seth's descendants had played the role of a lamp on the mountain for a long time.

. Messiah's lineage

Cain's descendants were the ancient civilization's founder in the genealogy of Genesis 4: farming, architecture, herding, music, and Bronze culture. They were the conqueror and rulers of the world. But they, being outside of Christ, were famous but turned out to be the serpent's seed. On the other hand, Seth's sons, being in Christ, were unknown in the world in the genealogy of Genesis 5 but turned out to be the woman's seed.

However, the comparison and contrast between two genealogies testify that Seth's descendants were more valuable than Cain's ones before God. Cain's genealogy was too simple. It was because those outside of Christ were no different from the beasts to perish before God (Ephesians 2:11-12). On the other hand, Seth's genealogy shows in detail when his descendants were born, how long they lived, and at what age they died. The protagonist of the world was not of Cain, but of Seth.

While Seth's sons lived a faithful life, God had shown mercy and grace upon humankind for 1,700 years until the judgment by the Flood. But the more the godliness of Seth's descendants collapsed, the faster God's patience came to an end. Therefore, Seth's sons' godliness enabled Cain's descendants to enjoy their lives for many years as powerful and famous in the world. However, the decrease of devout believers eventually made human society destroyed by the Flood.

Only Seth's descendants were of the Messiah's lineage, as promised in the Protoevangelium. His sons were sacred humanity. Enoch of his descendants ascended to Heaven by the faith in the Messiah to come. The Messiah was the center of secular and redemptive history. In the end, secular history and redemptive history could find an opportunity to exist only in Christ. It was because the Coming Messiah would be born out of the lineage of the woman's seed.

. Recipient and preacher of redemptive revelations

Modern theologians insist that the Pentateuch is a book composed of various materials and weaved by them together. The genealogy of Genesis 5 opposes this. Before the Flood, all the genealogical people had enjoyed a long life for almost one thousand years.

Before the Flood, Methuselah, as the seventh generation, lived together with Adam. It was a crucial fact for the transmission of biblical revelations. Adam and Eve were the first witnesses. The second witnesses were from Seth to Methuselah. All they lived together with Adam. Noah was born 126 years after Adam's death.

Lamech, Noah, and Shem were the third witnesses. However, they lived with the second witnesses for 100-600 years. The third witnesses were almost like the second ones. After the Flood, Noah and Shem delivered oral revelations to the future generations.

The current Revelations were God's Creation, cultural mission, Garden of Eden, the tree of good and evil knowledge, disobedience and Protoevangelium, deportation from the Garden of Eden, and Cain and Abel's life. The second witnesses knew them as well as the first ones.

Faith comes from listening to the Word of God (Rom. 10:17), and through faith, sinners can get the grace of justification (Rom.10:16-17). God took careful steps and wise measures to keep God's Words in excellent preservation. Abel, having heard only Genesis 1-3, became the first saint to be justified by faith.

The genealogy of Genesis 5 accurately recorded who inherited the Messiah's lineage promised in the original Gospel and testified who orally passed God's words down to future generations. There was no problem with the transmission of biblical revelations from generation to generation.

d.   **Flood**: Genesis 6-8 chapters

The Bible recorded Primeval History as the universal history of humanity until the 11th chapter of the Book of Genesis. And from the 12th chapter, the history of Israel, including Abraham's call, was recorded until the end of the Old Testament. So, the Old Testament consists of two representatives, Adam and Abraham. In other words, the Old Testament records both the universal history of humanity and the unique history of Israel, chosen people.

And the Primeval History of humankind is again divided into two representatives, Adam and Noah. Genesis 1-5 writes about Adam and his descendants, while Genesis 6-11 records about Noah and his descendants.

Noah was also a descendant of Adam. After Flood, however, Noah, like Adam, was another ancestor of a new humanity. He began to live in a new world that emerged after the Flood. But Noah, the new ancestor, could not be interpreted separately from Adam, the old ancestor.

There were both the continuity and discontinuity between Adam and Noah as follows:

		Adam	Noah
humanity	cause	Creation	salvation
	grace	Conditional after unconditional	
	content	New start	Re-start
	origin	From earth	
	status	Sinner	
Represen-tative	ancestor	Old	new
	Character	Universal	limited
	type	Jesus Christ	
covenant		Creation/redemption	preservation
world	content	Created	Re-created
	Character	Earthly	
Fall	cause	Eating forbidden fruit	Mixed marriage
	result	Noah's calling	Abram's calling
judgment	method	Expulsion from Eden	Flood
	result	Outside Divine covenant	

The Flood split the descendants of Adam and Noah into different humanity. However, all they belonged to Adam's bloody lineage. Noah's descendants also inherited the original sin committed by Adam. Noah's new world still belonged to Adam's old world, created by God.

Noah's new descendants were no different from Adam's ones. They were also under both the Covenants of Creation (Genesis 2:17) and Redemption (Genesis 3:15). However, the Flood made the two humanities quite different from each other. Noah's new world re-started or regenerated Adam's ancient world.

Noah needed to conclude a new covenant of preservation with God. There was a difference in Divine judgment between the covenants. The failure to keep the Creation covenant cut off the spiritual relationship with God, the Creator. But the redemptive covenant promised to restore the broken relationship.

However, the not-keeping of the redemptive covenant destroyed human society. There was no other redemption after the Flood. It means that the refusal of redemptive grace cannot presuppose another salvation. The rejection was to give up the opportunity for the fallen to live as a recreated human. This renunciation was the same as the unbelief in Christ, the Son of God, as the Redeemer. Such humanity, losing its worth before God, is no different from the beasts that will soon perish (Psalm 49:12, 20).

As shown above, the violation of the Creative covenant does not withdraw the common grace of God. He continues to show grace to fallen humankind (Deut. 32:33-35, Romans 2:5). Even the fallen world must have been preserved or maintained until achieving the purpose of Divine Creation. On the other hand, the rejection of the Redemptive covenant completely removes God's universal grace. God destroyed all the human being except for Noah's family.

However, both the Creation and Preservation covenants' rejections do not reap God's general grace, unlike the Redemptive covenant. The Creator cannot fail in the purpose of Creation (Genesis 1:26). And also, there still remains the elected to receive the grace of redemption among the fallen humanity.

In this respect, the great Flood pushed the old world to be re-started in a different form. God always makes each crisis changed into a new opportunity for Himself. It was because He already promised the Redemption for the achievement of Creative purpose.

God's Creation was for a new beginning, while Flood's judgment was for a renewed start. Divine judgment had a double meaning. It ended the age of the old covenant and opened the age of the new covenant. Naturally, there were continuity and discontinuity between the two covenants.

After the Flood, the new world was like the old world, as God's created world. And the new and old humanities were no different from each other, belonging to Adam's bloody lineage. It was why God, the Savior, repeatedly commanded Noah's new generation to keep the cultural mission (Genesis1:28).

"And God blessed Noah and his sons, and said unto them, Be fruitful, and multiply, and replenish the earth."(Genesis9:1)

The cultural mission aimed to build the Kingdom of God on earth. Even after the Flood, the purpose did not change. Humanity, saved from the Flood judgment, could participate again in the cultural mission. Only the grace of Redemption made a new start possible. God would preserve the renewed world and humanity by His unconditional grace until the final judgment by fire (Genesis 9:11-12). It was the goal of the covenant of preservation.

"But the heavens and the earth, which are now, by the same word are kept in store, reserved unto fire against the day of judgment and perdition of ungodly men."(2Peter3:7)

After the Flood, Noah became a renewed representative of humanity in the world. His righteous acts saved Adam's old humankind from the Flood judgment and enabled them to live in a re-generated world, as new humankind (Romans 5:18). He was a type of Christ, who will come as the second and last Adam.

But Noah was different from Christ. As prophesied in the original Gospel (Genesis 3:15), Noah's new human race, like Adam's old one, would also be divided into two, woman's seed and serpent's seed. How unique were the renewed world and redeemed humanity?

God's act of salvation restored from the fallen world to the re-created world. It renewed and brought back the lost in the Fall. In other words, only salvation makes the fallen stand before God again as re-created in God's image. Divine Redemption means not only physical salvation but also mental change.

Before the Flood, the fallen lived a life dominated by space in the old world. However, after the Flood, the redeemed had to live a life governed by time in the renewed earth. Therefore, the saved should live his new life by changing ideas, philosophy, and values.

In a word, Noah's new humankind had to live new mental energy in a renewed society. The Creation Article (Genesis 1-2) asserted that the visible material world was an eschatological existence governed by time, not by space. Noah's new world did not lose that character. Regenerated humankind also had to live an eschatological life.

And Adam was a created representative, while Noah – a redeemed one. In Adam, his descendants were born in God's image by God's action of Creation. Likewise, in Noah, his descendants were re-born in His image by God's act of salvation from the Flood. Similarly, the relationship between Adam and Noah was like that between Creation and redemption.

The created will attain his salvation after he becomes

redeemed. Likewise, Creation would reach its consummation through Redemption. But Creation first comes, and next Redemption. These double meanings had two truths.

Noah's re-started world was like a new world to be renewed by Christ's future deliverance. And the Post-Flood world, as well as the Pred-Flood world, had to need His future Redemption toward fulfillment and consummation.

Before the Flood, both the Old-Testamental Creation and Redemption revealed God's Kingdom in earthly symbols and types. There was no difference in it even after the Flood. The recreated humans were still subject to the same test as the created ones. Faith alone wins this test.

"But without faith [it is] impossible to please [him]: for he that cometh to God must believe that he is, and [that] he is a rewarder of them that diligently seek him."(Hebrew11:6)

Genesis 9-11 records Noah's descendants after the Flood. The history of new humankind consists of the followings; preservation covenant (verses 9:1-19), the genealogy of renewed humanity (verses 9:20-29), Eber and Nimrod (chapter 10), the Tower of Babel (verses 11:1-9), and Shem's genealogy (verses 11:10-32).

e. **Preservation Covenant**: Genesis 9:1-16

The work of Creation made it possible for nature to exist first in the universe, while the Flood Judgment – to restart the

페이지 **145 / 227**

already created world. Before signing the preservation covenant, God blessed the new humanity and commanded:

"And God blessed Noah and his sons, and said unto them, Be fruitful, and multiply, and replenish the earth. And the fear of you and the dread of you shall be upon every beast of the earth, and upon every fowl of the air, upon all that moveth [upon] the earth, and upon all the fishes of the sea; into your hand are they delivered." (Gen.9:1-2, 7)

The command, given to the new humanity after the Flood, was a repetition of the cultural mandate (Genesis1:28) given to Adam and Eve after the Creation. In this respect, Noah's covenant of Preservation was an extension of Adam's covenant of Creation. Like the covenant of Creation, the covenant of Preservation emphasized the unconditional grace of God. Both created and saved humankind unconditionally received God's mercy and grace.

However, there were also differences between the two. The Pred-Creational cultural mission (Genesis 1:28) presupposed close cooperation between human society and natural creatures. However, the Post-Flood cultural mission (Genesis 9:1-2) did not meet it. Adam's Fall and Cain's first murder made the land further cursed. The curse remained the same as ever after the Flood.

Nature heals itself by the principle of circulation. However, the land, its insects, and animals would not help the Post-Flood cultural mission of humankind. The discord between humans and animals would badly impact this principle of circulation. However, the covenant of Creation (Genesis 1:28) and the covenant of Redemption (Genesis 3:15) will remain in effect thanks to the Preservation covenant (Genesis 9:9-17).

"And God said, This [is] the token of the covenant which I make between me and you and every living creature that [is] with you, for perpetual generations: I do set my bow in the cloud, and it shall be for a token of a covenant between me and the earth. And it shall come to pass, when I bring a cloud over the earth, that the bow shall be seen in the cloud: And I will remember my covenant, which [is] between me and you and every living creature of all flesh; and the waters shall no more become a flood to destroy all flesh. And the bow shall be in the cloud; and I will look upon it, that I may remember the everlasting covenant between God and every living creature of all flesh that [is] upon the earth." (Gen.9:12-16)

There was also one more difference between the two covenants. People ate vegetables before the Flood (Genesis 1:29-31), but they additionally began to eat meats after the Flood.

"And the fear of you and the dread of you shall be upon every beast of the earth, and upon every fowl of the air,

upon all that moveth [upon] the earth, and upon all the fishes of the sea; into your hand are they delivered. Every moving thing that liveth shall be meat for you; even as the green herb have I given you all things. But flesh with the life thereof, [which is] the blood thereof, shall ye not eat. And surely your blood of your lives will I require; at the hand of every beast will I require it, and at the hand of man; at the hand of every man's brother will I require the life of man. Whoso sheddeth man's blood, by man shall his blood be shed: for in the image of God made he man."(Gen.9:2-6)

It was clear that the ecosystem underwent a tremendous change. The Flood opened the way of eating meats, as inevitable nutrition for survival in a new world.

However, unlike the Pred-Flood, between man and beasts arouse hostility and discord instead of the bond, intimacy, and peace. The closeness, as the cause of the Fall, had utterly disappeared.

But Fall's incident demanded a carnivore diet. Then, God warned them not to eat meat with blood because blood was life itself. Shedding the blood of a person in the image of God was strictly forbidden. If so, God would ask for the murderer's blood. It was because nobody should spill human blood carelessly except for a redemptive purpose. God revealed the more advanced doctrine of redemption (Genesis 3:21, 4:4).

And after the Fall, the more peoples rejected the faith in the Creation and Redemption, the more prevalent their evil and injustice became in society. God, knowing about it, forbade people not to shed humane blood except redemption.

At this moment, God newly taught them ransom death. The Flood judgment testifies that death was the price of sin. They got a new life through salvation from Flood's death. Their continual survival, however, also required ransom sacrifice. Seeing this need, they had to take care of the herds. After the Flood, cattle-ranching life became as meaningful and vital as agricultural life.

Noah, having gone forth out of the ark, built an altar unto the Lord. Taking every clean beast and fowl, he offered burnt offerings on the altar (Genesis8:19-21). Thanking God's salvation from the Flood also required redemptive death.

For a while, farming was impossible after the Flood. Humankind had to wait for the earth to dry. Until this time, they solved the problem of foods with the livestock from the ark. They killed herds every day. Every time they spilled the blood of beasts upon the ground and finally could get food. Thus, they remembered in every meal that only the ransom death gave them the food to prolong re-born life in a renewed world.

The ark stopped on Mount Ararat. New humans slowly moved to the east. It was only in the field of Shinar of Mesopotamia that they were able to get farming started (Gen. 11:2). Until this time, they could get meats thanks to pastures. Thus, God mercifully helped them better realize the importance of future redemption by the Coming Messiah.

f.   **Shem, Ham, and Japheth**: Genesis 9:18-29

Shortly after leaving the ark, Noah planted a vine (Genesis 9:20). The Hebraic version of this verse follows; Noah, the man of the earth, started and grew a vine. The man of the land means that he, being out of the soil, is a farmer. The cursed by the Fall had to live by farming again.

The descendants of Noah's three sons spread out over the world until they reached the plains of Shinar (Gen. 9:19). For a while, grape farming was more manageable than grain farming after the Flood. It was enough to plant vines that sprout and grow on slopes or in stony fields. They were able to grow grapes as much as he could take care of the animals for food and sacrifice.

After the harvest, Noah made and drank wine. Being drunken and naked, he fell asleep in the tent. There was nothing wrong with Noah's behavior. However, there happened a filial problem with the three sons. And their attitude toward Noah determined their futures.

A person's actions reflect what way of thinking he has. People's thinking shows what kind of thoughts, philosophy, and values they accumulate in their minds. The amassed knowledge forms the fixed way of thinking, and they judge and act accordingly. Thus, they are going to shape their future life.

Therefore, God judges people by their thoughts, philosophy, and values, not by their outward actions (1 Sam. 16:7, Prov. 16:2, Rev. 2:23). It was why Noah could not easily ignore the three sons' ethical behavior toward himself.

The faith in God, the Creator, willingly accepts the lessons from the Creation Article (Genesis 1-2), and it helps form the ideas, philosophy, and values fitting a biblical perspective. Accordingly, time, not space, dominates saints' view of the world and history. The visible world does not influence them. Its phenomena do not shake believers in creationism, either.

However, the denial of belief in the Creator makes people rely on space, not time. Atheists become obsessed with materialism. The visible world influences their ideas, philosophy, and values. Even though they also show a very high and noble level of logical beauty, their philosophy and values, denying the Creator, are like lies-worshiping idolatry.

How did Noah's three sons say about themselves?

Canaan first saw Noah's nakedness. Ham was the father of Canaan (Genesis 9:18). Canaan was the youngest as Ham's fourth son (1 Chronicle 1:8). At the same time, Canaan was Noah's grandson. When the three sons worked, Canaan, remaining in the tent, accidentally saw grandfather drunken and naked. Canaan went to Ham, his father, and told him about his grandfather.

Ham went to check and saw his father's lower body. He went outside and told Shem and Japheth about father (Genesis 9:22). The Hebrew word for 'tell' means to speak openly rather than quietly. Having heard from him, Shem and Japheth put clothes on the shoulders and stepped back to cover the father's nakedness (v. 23).

In comparison with Shem and Japheth, there was an ethical problem with Ham and Canaan. If Canaan had respected Noah, his grandfather, he should have secretly covered Noah's shame above all. Ham should have behaved like that. However, he looked at the father's nakedness on purpose. And he sarcastically said it to his brothers. Ham did not honor his father at all like his son Canaan (Ephesians 6:2).

Ham was not a filial son. His unfilial attitude toward Noah might have a bad influence on his son, Canaan. Canaan also scornfully said about Noah to his father, Ham. Ham's family education revealed the wrong effect. Like Canaan, also grew up Ham's other sons: Cush, Mizraim, Put.

After the Flood, Noah became a new human ancestor, like Adam. Their salvation from the Flood judgment was possible thanks to Noah's righteousness. And also, he was the head of the family. Noah, as the representative of humanity, was like the Messiah with three offices: king, priest, and prophet.

He was qualified to deserve respect from his sons. They had to learn from the life of Noah, their father, and teach his descendants. However, Ham failed this. His unfilial resulted from the unbelief in God, the Savior. Accordingly, Ham and his children behaved themselves ungodly before God. Noah might have known about it as well.

Having awakened up, Noah heard the behaviors of his sons.

Noah declared a blessing and a curse corresponding to his sons' filial level as the new ancestor.

Canaan would be cursed and become slaves to his brothers (v. 25). On the other hand, Noah called God, the Savior from the Flood, as the God of Shem (v. 26). It was because Shem took the initiative in having covered up his father's shame. And Japheth was willing to help his elder brother. God will enlarge Japheth and let him dwell in the tents of Shem (v. 27).

Jehovah, God of the covenant, became the God of Shem. God will conclude a new covenant with Shem's descendants, who inherited the Covenants of Creation, Redemption, and Preservation. In the future, the children of Japheth will enjoy the grace of God in Shem's tent. On the other hand, Ham and Canaan's children will be slaves to those of Shem and Japheth.

Noah's incident occurred between the signing of the Preservation covenant (Gen. 9) and the human lineage (Gen. 10). The new covenant said about God's grace upon the new humanity, but the human genealogy - the new humankind's flourishment on earth.

The lives of Noah and his three sons had both spiritual (religious) and social (ethical) meanings. The Old Testament always teaches faith and love together. Love without faith or faith without love is detestable before God.

There was nothing wrong with Noah's behavior. However, there was a problem with the attitude of the children toward it. In this test, Shem and Japheth won, while Ham and Canaan failed. In this way, their future revealed itself differently from one another. Only faith in God with love for neighbors will make saints stand before God as one of His glorious sons.

    g.   **Two cultures at war** (2)

Cain, who killed Abel, his younger brother, settled in Nod. The settlement meant an agricultural life. Over time, they founded the ancient civilization of humankind. Before the Flood, Cain's descendants ruled the world. Cain's agricultural experience taught that the denial of Creation faith led to temporal hedonism.

On the other hand, Seth's descendants, godly people, lived in nature as nomads. Compared with them, Cain's sons settled in the castle and lived a comfortable life. Seth's descendants were poor and weak in the world. They lived an ascetic life for a while, but they gradually joined the agricultural life, which gave Cain's descendants economic wealth and pleasing comfort.

Evil and injustice prevailed in the world. It was the leading cause of the Flood judgment. Satan and Cain's descendants seemingly triumphed in the spiritual battle. However, God destroyed Adam's old humanity by Flood, and God started again with Noah's new humankind. In the end, God triumphed.

4.   **Babel Tower**

Noah's new humanity of Post-Flood was essentially no different from Adam's old humankind of Pred-Flood. As prophesied in the Protoevangelium, Noah's new descendants will also split into two spiritual groups: the woman's seed and the serpent's seed. This division and struggle had appeared in the genealogy of the 10th chapter of the book of Genesis.

A spiritual battle already arose among the Hamites, Semites, and Japhethites. They already revealed the conflict in their attitude toward Noah, their father (Genesis 9:20-29). In such a state of competition, the Tower of Babel made single humanity scattered over the world by language and nation.

a.   **Nimrod and Eber**: Genesis 10 chapter

In the genealogy of Chapter 10 were well noted two main characters: Nimrod, the sixth youngest son of Cush, Ham's eldest son (Genesis 10:8), and Eber, the third generation of Shem (vs. 10:24-25, 11:14).

Ham was an unfilial son to his father, Noah, while Shem was a filial son. Their ethical attitude determined whether or not they inherited the faith of Noah, their father. Ham rejected the faith, while Shem inherited it. Likewise, the same thing happened with Hamites and Semites, respectively.

Hamites were very prosperous. Fifteen verses introduced the Hamites through verses 6-20. However, eleven verses recorded the Semites through verses 21-31, whereas four verses said about the Japhethites through verses 2-5. It might suppose that the Hamites prospered one third more than the Semites and nearly four times more than the Japhethites.

At that time, the sons of Ham were relatively powerful. They lived in the Shinar of Mesopotamia and flourished. When the Semites and Japhethites lived a mainly nomadic life, the Hamites blossomed agrarian culture and became rulers of the world. The sons of Shem and Japheth, different in spiritual disposition, further got away from Ham's sons. And the non-settled nomadic culture could not get along with the settled agricultural culture. Nomads usually lived around the village, not in its center.

Nimrod, the youngest son of Cush, Ham's eldest son, became the world's mighty one. The proverb of those times said, **"No one is an unusual hunter before the Lord like Nimrod."** (Genesis 10:9) Septuagint, a Greek translation of the Old Testament, paraphrases the expression **before Jehovah** as against Jehovah. And his name came from the Hebrew verb 'to rebel.'   He gradually became famous among people. Considering the infidelity and unbelief of the Ham family, Nimrod was a worldly hero against Jehovah. Specifically, he was a hunter.

In many ways, hunting was utterly different from shepherding. Hunting catches or kills wild animals in mountains and fields while shepherding takes care of livestock. Hunting slaughters with weapons while shepherding protects the cattle with rod or stick.

Furthermore, hunting life happily goes against nature, while shepherding life tries to get along with nature. Hunting is a fun-pursuing hobby while shepherding is a sacrificing service. And hunting requires selfish violence, while shepherding - altruistic devotion.

Hunter in agricultural life was utterly different from the shepherd in the nomadic one. At that time, hunters enjoyed world popularity, while shepherds had nothing to do with the world's favor.

People gathered around Nimrod, the world's first hero. In those days, people had lived for an average of 500 years until the incident of Babel Tower. During his survival time, Nimrod was able to expand his power sufficiently. Over time, Nimrod became the ruler of the world.

He established an agricultural society on the plains of Shinar, together with his fellow Hamites. The community grew bigger and bigger and became an empire. His kingdom began in Babel, Erech, Accad, and Calneh in Shinar's land, and then went to Ashur and built cities in Nineveh, Rehoboth, Calah, and Resen between Nineveh and Calah (v. 11-12). He became the founder of the ancient Babylonian Empire. The Hamites seized the domination of the world.

Farming culture aims for a settled society. Collective farming life is needed. In its turn, a collective-settled organization pursues totalitarian or authoritarian governance. A ruler can easily concentrate his powers, and he builds as many castles as possible and conducts territorial conquests to enlarge his powers.

The central government system with concentrated power

facilitates the mobilization of collective labor and military power. When the ruler succeeds in expanding his empire, he meets other temptations. By exalting himself as a divine being, he desires the absolute power that only God can enjoy. The marriage between politics and religion makes it possible.

When a ruler becomes a god, he initiates large-scale civil works. It is to build a city with a huge temple where people worship him (Genesis11). The ruler wastes enormous national power and resources enough to weaken and endanger his empire itself eventually. All this is the result of rejecting the faith in God, the Creator.

Nimrod denied the Creator God (Genesis 1-2) and opposed the Redeemer, promised in the Protoevangelium. He was one of the Hamites, who were unwilling to have faith in Creation and Redemption. He served as an antichrist in favor of atheism. Here were several characteristics of the advent of antichrist Nimrod.

Antichrist was close at hand. The original Gospel (Genesis 3:15) had already revealed who the serpent's seed was. The seed means a group that spiritually follows Satan, who had disguised himself as a serpent.

Nimrod went hunting in the mountains and fields rather than staying in the house. Excellent hunting skills made him a hero before the people. He very much enjoyed the world population. The more he did, the more he went farther away from God, the Creator.

As Nimrod grew up, he became more and more powerful.

After taking power among people, he established a country and became its ruler. Nimrod began to stand openly against God, the Creator, and became an antichrist as a seed of the serpent. At that time, Noah and other Witnesses of the Flood still lived.

The account of Nimrod in Genesis 10 reveals that antichrists can appear at any time, even after the Flood. Evil still existed and worked in the new world. Nimrod, as an antichrist, came out of the sons of Noah, a new ancestor. Later, Apostle John said that antichrists went out of us (1 John 2:18-19).

Antichrist emerged as a hero. Many people admired him. To this end, he tried to boast of his extraordinary gift. He loved the glory of the world. And when he succeeded in it, he openly opposed God, the Creator. It was for himself to rise to the position of God. As a wicked dictator, he adopted politics against God.

Nimrod was different from Moses. Moses, the prince of ancient Egypt, was able to become Pharaoh. However, he did not seek the glory, respect, and honor of the world. He humbled himself, thinking about the sufferings of his people.

And antichrist used hedonism. The hunters catch beasts for a living. At the same time, they hunt for entertainment. Hunting becomes lifelong entertainment. The entertainer pursues fun for himself. The joy of hunting is a selfish pleasure. Having seized world power, Nimrod sought a different form of worldly pleasure. He changed the target of hunting from beasts to people. Thus, he went away further from God, the Creator, and Redeemer.

After he became the leader of the people, he completely abandoned God. He thought that the Flood was a natural phenomenon and denied the Lordship of God, the Creator. The denial gave him the freedom to do whatever he wanted.

Meanwhile, what did the sons of Shem and Japheth do at this time?

Shem, as Noah's eldest son, witnessed the Flood judgment, and he passed on Noah's faith. Noah already declared that God, the Creator, would be the Lord, God of Shem (Genesis 9:26). Over time, Shem became known as the father of all the children of Eber (Genesis10:21). It means that the descendants of Eber passed on Shem's faith. And the Semitic genealogy (v. 21) also introduced Shem as the brother of Japheth. The children of Japheth, along with the children of Eber, participated sufficiently in Semitic faith.

The Semites lived in the lower stream of Mesopotamia, east of the settlements of Ham and Japheth. They well understood that the cause of the Flood lay in the settled agricultural life subordinate to space. They preferred a nomadic life to an agricultural one. And they lived around the farming society, not at its center. The Semites were different in this from the Hamites.

After the Flood, Noah lived another 350 years. He always lived life in a tent (Genesis 9:21). They chose the temporal way of thinking rather than the spatial way of thinking. Semites believed in Creation (Genesis 1-2) and lived in hope for Redemption (Genesis 3:15). The nomadic life fitted to the creative faith better than the agricultural one.

This nomadic life of faith had become stronger and stronger since the birth of Eber, the third generation of Shem (Genesis 10:21). Peleg was born when Eber was 34 years old (Gen. 11:16). At this time, Noah's descendants spread all over the world.

During 34 years between Eber and Peleg, God spiritually blessed the Semites through Eber. Semitic faith in the Creation and Redemption met a period of revival mainly among the children of Eber. In those days, Nimrod, Ham's grandson, tried to build up the Tower of Babel. The Hamites happily joined it, while the Semites and Japhethites had to leave the Hamites. The Japhethites moved to the Anatoli Peninsula's southern coastal region, while the Semites - to the south of the lower Mesopotamia.

Most of the Semites were supposed to live agricultural life except Noah and Shem, the Flood judgment's primary witnesses. Noah lived until Abram's birth. And Shem, Arphaxad, Salah and Eber survived even after his birth. While the Hamites held the world's reign, these six Semites helped ignite and sustain the creative and redemptive faith.

The genealogy in Genesis 10 chapter pointed out that Nimrod, the youngest grandson of Ham, was the protagonist of the Tower of Babel incident (Genesis 10:9-12). On the other hand, it implies that Eber, the third generation of Shem, was the vanguard of the faith movement in the era of disbelief.

In those days, a spiritual conflict arose between the Hamites and Semites. At this time, the Japhethites joined the Semites. Thus, Noah's children spiritually split into the woman's seed and the serpent's seed.

And they philosophically divided themselves into two ways of thinking: temporal thinking and spatial thinking. The first demanded a nomadic life from the Semites, but the second required an agricultural one from the Hamites.

After the Flood, many of the Semites continued to live life in a tent. On the other hand, the Hamites built a castle and lived a hedonistic life. As a result, the Hamites were famous in the world, but the Semites were unknown.

The Semites and Hamites after the Flood were precisely like the descendants of Seth and Cain before the Flood. It is clear evidence that there are both the continuity and discontinuity or the repetition and development of biblical revelations.

b. **The incident of Babel Tower**: Genesis 11:1-9

The flat land of Shinar belongs to the Mesopotamian region between the two rivers of Euphrates and Tigris. It was the best area for farming. After the Flood, Ham's descendants built up the first settled society based on agricultural life there.

And they began to set up the Tower of Babel around the lifetime of Eber, and when he gave birth to Peleg (Genesis 10:25), all they dispersed and spread across the world by the

Divine curse (Genesis11:1-9). It happened about 130 years after the Flood. As Adam's sons, Noah's new humankind was also quick to disobey God, the Creator.

At the time, Nimrod was the first mighty hunter in the world. Seeking and enjoying world populations, he rejected the faith in the Creator and Redeemer more than ever. And the agricultural culture of the Shinar Plains strengthened his world power sufficiently.

They advanced to Ashur and built castles here and there. Thus, he established the ancient Babylonian empire. And he needed a symbol to perpetuate his power. It was why the children of Ham tried to build a tower at Babel under the rulership of Nimrod.

"And they said one to another, Go to, let us make brick, and burn them throughly. And they had brick for stone, and slime had they for morter. And they said, Go to, let us build us a city and a tower, whose top [may reach] unto heaven; and let us make us a name, lest we be scattered abroad upon the face of the whole earth."(Genesis11:3-4)

The purpose of the construction was to avoid scattering by making a name for humans, not for God. This purpose directly opposed the cultural mandate (Genesis 1:28) to fill the earth together with human growth and prosperity. By bringing the top of the tower up to the sky, Nimrod tried to spread his name. He wanted to make a building indestructible even in a flood-like judgment. The Tower of Babel was a brilliant symbol of humanism and heroism.

God had already promised not to judge the world with water again (Genesis 9:11). Until the final decision by fire, there would be no more judgments to destruct humanity. But Nimrod and his peoples intentionally wanted to prepare for another flood judgment. The Tower of Babel aimed to completely oppose and neutralize God, the Creator, and His judgment. The Tower was clear evidence of disbelief in the Creator.

At this moment, most of the Semites and Japhethites were unable to participate in Nimrod's unbelief movement. The Japhethites migrated to the Anatolian Peninsula's shores to the northwest, and the Semites descended further southeast, that is, downstream of Mesopotamia. It was why Abraham had to leave Ur of Chaldea to go to Canaan, the promised land.

God could no longer condone his efforts to construct the Tower of Babel. The main motive for betrayal was that Noah's descendants still used one language to communicate. God cursed them and caused them to speak different languages to make them scattered around the world by nations (Genesis 11:6-7). Nimrod had to stop Castle building abruptly (verse 9).

Settled farming society made it possible to build the Tower of Babel, a symbol of humanism and atheism. Agricultural culture eventually enabled Nimrod to concentrate his political power. In its turn, the concentration also facilitated the workforce's mobilization to construct the Tower of Babel.

For this, he incorporated religion into politics. He exalted himself as a god and forced the people to worship him. Thus, Nimrod ruled with his own words, ignoring the Creator and His orders. The Ham family's unbelief was very much blossomed by the Tower of Babel but in failure.

Fundamentally, agricultural life makes people get caught in space, not in time. Accordingly, peoples like to live together, forming a settled community. And they make endless efforts to overcome nature to get more wealth. The ruler easily deifies power, and the people willingly venerate material. Tyranny and idolatry usually characterize agricultural life.

However, nomadic culture characterizes unsettlement. People live scattered for survival. To be compared with the agricultural society, shepherding society relies upon nature for further survival.

People are more conscious of divine existence in nature. The ways of thinking and living in the nomadic community are closer to the Divine creation belief. Nomadic people could find three monotheistic religions in the world: Judaism, Muslims, and Christianity.

God, the Creator, had to start anew to achieve the purposes of Creation and Redemption. To this end, God scattered humanity all over the world. Afterward, He chose one of the scattered nations. It was why Primeval History recorded Shem's genealogy immediately after the incident of Babel Tower.

c. **The last event of the Primeval History**

Until now, the interpretation of the event of Babel Tower has meanings symbolical or didactical. But it is secondary teaching. The primary instruction is that the Tower of Babel symbolizes the unbelief and humanism that reject God, the Creator, and the Redeemer. Rejectors begin to think that he would only hope for this visible world.

From then on, their thinking is subordinated to space, not time, and leads them to live a closed life on a spatial way of thinking. It is the same result from eating the fruit of good and evil knowledge.

Human society becomes more and more obsessed with the agricultural community. When human beings control a nation as sinners before God, the corruptible leader always dominates society. The government would be a humane kingdom, but not God's Kingdom. And its governor would dictate the country by his virtues, not by God's words. Human society tends to choose totalitarianism and tyranism as a system of government. The future of human society is as evident as you see a fire.

Humanism rejecting the Creator's faith always has an illusion that humans will resolve everything in their goodness and power. It asserts ideas, philosophy, and values, which lead them to failure, defeat, and final destruction. The Primeval History (Genesis-11) already revealed the future of human civilization and culture.

The Old Testament did not mention universal humanity anymore from the 12th chapter of Genesis. However, God, the Creator, had to continue His work. To this end, the Creator will reveal Himself as the Redeemer. Significantly, the chosen and redeemed by God will be able to build the kingdom of God in this world. This way, God will show the world the exact difference between the rules by God's law and by humane virtues.

d. **Shem's genealogy**: Genesis 11:10-32

The genealogy showed the Messiah's bloody lineage from Shem, the Flood's primary witness, to Abram, his ninth generation. Shem had five sons: Elam, Asshur, Arphaxad, Lud, and Aram. Arphaxad, the third son, succeeded the bloody lineage of the Messiah to come.

The 10th chapter of Genesis did not record Reu, Peleg's son, but Joktan, the brother of Peleg, while the 11th chapter of Genesis showed Reu, Peleg's son but not Joktan. It means that the genealogy of Chapter 10 only introduces universal humanity, as the descendants of Noah. However, the genealogy of Chapter 11 primarily records the bloody linage of the Messiah to come.

The first genealogy was recorded after the Flood, while the second one – after the incident of Babel Tower. In this respect, the two genealogies are very different from each other. However, the two have a common thing in that two lineages belong to Adam's genealogy.

Therefore, Shem's genealogy testifies that Abraham, the ancestor of Israel, was out of Adam's family and out of the lineage of woman's seed, as well. Abraham was the heir of all the covenants of Creation, Redemption, and Preservation. However, Noah's descendants, other than Abraham, were out of the redemptive covenant.

This genealogy tells that Noah, the Flood's primary witness, lived until Terah, and Shem lived after Abraham's birth, Terah's son. And Eber, who inherited Shem's faith (Genesis 10:21), survived during Abraham's life. Both Eber and Terah saw Noah and Shem in their lifetime. Terah and Abram knew about the faith-revival movement by Eber and his descendants.

Before the Flood, Noah and Shem orally heard from their ancestors the revelations until the 5th chapter of Genesis. After the Flood, Noah and Shem lived for 350 and 500 years, respectively. They had enough time orally to tell their descendants about biblical narratives until Genesis 11: Creation, Fall, Redemption, Flood, and Babel Tower. Thus, the Primeval History (Genesis 1-11), as biblical revelations, was orally handed down from generation to generation by Noah, Shem, and their children.

The average life span exceeded 400 years from Arphaxad to Eber, and from Peleg to Serug, about 200 years. Nahor, Terah, and Abram respectively lived no more than 200 years. Most of the descendants of Shem had enough time to acquaint with the biblical narratives very well.

The Primeval History was a form of a historical narrative so that people might easily remember God's Words. Above all,

Protoevangelium (Genesis3:15) was the Gospel itself as Divine prophecy and promise of the Coming Messiah. Any people who believed in the promised Redemption of Protoevangelium would get salvation. There remained only a difference in the redemption preemptive or fulfilled.

The genealogy of Genesis 10 shows the linage of universal humanity. This genealogy mentioned the Tower of Babel. Whereas the genealogy of Chapter 11 shows the genealogy of Abraham, the ancestor of Israel. This genealogy did not record the Tower of Babel. However, chapter 11 recorded both the Tower of Babel incident and Shem's genealogy together.

The Tower of Babel belonged to secular history, but it had something to do with the redemptive one. It meant that the incident of Babel Tower was the leading cause for Abraham's calling from God, the Creator. Abraham was the last of the characters recorded in Shem's genealogy.

The genealogy of Genesis chapter 11 foretells that the narrative of redemption will break with secular history. However, the redemptive narration still had its roots in secular history because Primeval History belongs to humanity's universal history.

The Shem genealogy reveals two contradicting facts. On the one hand, redemptive history inherited secular history. On the other hand, the first separated itself from the latter. The two records have both homogeneity and heterogeneity.

Abraham's private life inherited the Divine mission to construct God's kingdom on earth, oriented and targeted by the Primeval History. However, his life's narrative was utterly different from secular history to establish a humane and earthly realm.

The continuity and discontinuity between them did not teach the complete separation of his life's narrative from secular history. Israel, the descendant of Abraham, cannot claim that they are only a nation chosen by God in the world. They are also Adam's descendants, as sinners before God.

However, Shem's genealogy also testifies that Abraham, the father of Israel, belongs to the bloody lineage of the woman's seed. The redemptive revelations will be continually given to Israel, the heir of the covenants: Creation, Redemption, and Preservation. Suddenly Abram destroyed the idols of his father, Terah (Joshua 24:2). Shem's genealogy testifies that Abraham's conversion was inevitable, not accidental.

The average life span was 400 years until Eber, Noah's fourth generation. After the Flood, Noah survived 350 years, Shem 399 years, Arphaxad 339 years, Selah 369 years, and Eber, Peleg's father, 430 years, respectively. The incident of Babel Tower occurred 130 years after the Flood. Most of the Semites, including Noah, witnessed the incident.

Before the Flood, Noah and Shem lived in the ancient world. Shem had seen Methuselah and Lamech firsthand for nearly 100 years until the Flood. Noah and Shem were third-generation Witnesses who indirectly received the revelations from Adam.

At the same time, they were direct witnesses of the Flood. After the Flood, they became the first witnesses in the delivery of Bible revelations. Shem also was a living witness of the original Gospel, as was Noah.

Abram might have met Noah and Shem for at least 50 years before his leaving for Canaan. Someday in his past, Abram must have heard firsthand about the actual redemptive events of Pre-Flood and also Post-Flood. It was the reason why Abram suddenly converted to God, the Creator (Joshua 24:2-3).

Abram belonged to the fourth generation to succeed Adam in the delivery of Bible revelations. About 2,000 years already passed from Adam to Abram. However, the divine revelations passed through only three generations unto the fourth generation. It was as if the first-generation witness had delivered directly to the fourth generation. Contrary to common sense, the revelations were in vivid preservation and succession.

Abram heard and believed the Bible revelations up to Genesis 11 chapter. It was wonderful and beautiful that he could get justified by faith, having listened to the revelations recorded in the 11 chapters of Genesis (Romans 10:17). The Primeval History (Genesis 1-11) was so crucial as biblical revelations. The Protoevangelium (Genesis 3:15) was of particular importance among the revelations.

Abraham left for Canaan about 600 years later after the

Flood or nearly 500 years later after the incident of Babel Tower. Abram's sudden conversion also helped convert his father, Terah. They gave up idol-worship, left for Canaan, and stayed in Haran on the way there (Gen. 11:31). It was because of his old father. After having lived in Haran for a while, Abram again left for Canaan.

Then, he was 75 years old (Genesis 12:4). His departure on a long and dangerous road to Canaan was clear evidence that he realized the redemptive meaning hidden in the Primitive history and Protoevangelium (Genesis3:15). Abram just followed the word of the Lord (Genesis 12:4).

"By faith Abraham, when he was called to go out into a place which he should after receive for an inheritance, obeyed; and he went out, not knowing whither he went."(Heb.11:8)

e. Two Cultures at War (3)

After the Flood, Eber and Nimrod respectively represented the current flow of religion and ideology. Eber was out of Shem, while Nimrod - out of Ham. Eber believed in God, the Creator, and the future Redemption, while Nimrod ignored and rejected both. Eber and his descendants, possessing eschatological faith, lived a nomadic life. However, Nimrod, choosing temporal hedonism, lived an agricultural life.

Apocalyptic beliefs have led to the temporal way of thinking but present hedonism - the spatial way of thinking. The latter seemingly was the winner. Nimrod could accumulate power and wealth through agricultural culture and, at last, built an empire. And he made himself admired as a god. The farming culture enabled political totalitarianism and the religious deification of dictator.

Later, God made Nimrod a loser by stopping the construction of the Babel Tower. In front of men, the Hamites first looked like a victor. But before God, the Semites were the real victors.

After the Fall, the rebellion level of human society became higher and higher. First, Cain **privately** killed Abel. Next, Cain's descendants were **culturally** superior to Seth's ones. In those days, injustice and evil were rampant. And after the Flood, humanity, by building the Tower of Babel, made Nimrod a victor **politically and religiously**.

God had repeatedly neutralized the evil and unrighteous schemes of individuals as well as society. And God mocked the world's victors by judging the human companies which were corruptible religiously and politically. The Creator also served as the judge.

In this world, spiritual battles continue in the social fields of culture, ideology, politics, and religion. Atheism seems to triumph for a while, but creationism always wins in the end.

5. **Other meanings of Primeval History**

The diagram below shows the logical structure of the Primeval History (Genesis 1-11):

Main theme		Kingdom of God				
Chris-tology	identity	Christ the Son of God before incarnation				
	who	Creator		Redeemer		Judge
Ance-stor	1	Adam				
	2	Adam/start				Noah/re-start
	2-1	Adam		Seth		Noah
His-tory	theme	Creation				
	event	Crea-tion	Fall			
	Cove-nant	Creation		Redemption		Preser-vation
	Narra-tive	Crea-tion	Fall	Mixed Marriage	Flood	Babel Tower

Primeval History was not a myth, but history itself. It began with Creation Article (Genesis 1-2), that should be historical. God the Creator had revealed himself by the Divine creation of the visible world.

a. Theology and science/faith and reason

The act of God's Creation embodied theology as a science on the natural world. Of course, there is a difference between them. Theology is men's study of God by faith, while science –

their review of the natural world by reason. In the Creative record, however, there's no conflict between theology and science or between faith and reason.

The Christian Bible explains the relationship between the invisible Creator and all His visible creatures only by a logical dichotomy, but not by a confrontational one. The latter leads to abandoning either the Creator or the natural world. However, the logical dichotomy takes both with the help of logical order. God, the Creator, logically precedes the natural world.

The Creator, being spiritual, revealed Himself through the natural world. Otherwise, God could not reveal Himself. However, the Creator and His activities are invisible, and the natural world, as His creations, is visible. Man's relationship between spirit and body helps explain the relationship between the Creator and His creatures.

Spirit gives personality and animal life to the body. Without him, the body loses its psychical and animal vitality. Thus, the spirit makes himself known by the body. He needs flesh for himself.

God had created the natural world to realize His rule in human society. Toward this goal, the Creator should always work to keep the natural world and human society in good preservation and regular maintenance with His Words.

The denial of the Creation belief forces confrontational dichotomy to replace logical one. From then on, humanity prefers nature, science, and reason to the Creator, theology, and faith. Men become the master of all things, and science and reasoning become the worldly ruling principles. Naturally, men's ideas, philosophy, and values are based on dualism, pantheism, and deism in human society.

As mentioned above, the Bible does not ignore reason and science. The belief in Divine Creation does not neglect the historical fact and its phenomena at all. The presence and manifestations also reflect the providential will and wish of the Creator.

Following the logical dichotomy, the Creation article just emphasizes theology and faith more than science and reason. Faith and theology help people more deeply apprehend the world, nature and their happenings than reason and common sense. It is because reason, denying the confidence in the Creation, cannot understand them beyond the phenomena.

God, using natural methods, delivered the special revelations to His people. Without faith, however, natural revelations cannot interpret special revelations of the Bible. The only reason, reborn of faith, can make it possible. Then, the natural revelations help better understand the special revelations.

b. **Redemptive history and secular history**

The History transmitted the redemptive revelations in humankind's universal history until the 11th chapter of Genesis's book. For a while, the redemptive history had been inclusive in a secular one. They could not separate themselves from each other.

From Genesis 12, the universal history of humanity ended,

and the chosen people's history began. The Bible excluded the secular history of universal humanity. It seemed that God worked in humankind's universal history until Genesis 11 and no longer would work after Chapter 12.

The divine economy had changed. The same God would work on different historical stages. God would continually deliver the redemptive revelations in the chosen people's history as in the Primeval History. And the purpose of constructing God's Kingdom would remain the same as ever.

God would choose one of the human races to achieve His creative goal. Only the redeemed by God's grace could become a citizen of that Kingdom. Why was universal human history no longer recorded after Genesis 11 in the Bible? The Primeval History revealed the content, character, and method of secular history thoroughly enough to interpret the future secular one. It would be possible to study human history by learning the Primeval History of the Bible.

The Primeval History was the starting point of the chosen people's history, recorded from Genesis 12. The latter history was an extension of the first one. The chosen people were also the descendants of Adam's lineage and sinners in need of God's redemption. The chosen people's history would advance toward the future similarly to the Primeval History. Protology predicted eschatology.

The Primeval History showed various spiritual struggles between the woman's seed and serpent's seed, as predicted in the Protoevangelium: Cain and Abel, the families of Cain and Seth, the sons of God and the daughters of men, and the

Semites and Hamites.

Those similar struggles would continually occur between universal humankind and chosen people. In every case, God worked and would work in various ways to protect the chosen people belonging to the woman's seed.

As prophesied in the Protoevangelium, the secular history always opposed the redemptive one. It also served God's purpose. The redemptive history was like a town shining on the hill, while secular history - a city under the mountain. This privilege was the hidden glory of redemptive history, always persecuted in the world.

The redemptive history helps the secular history see the light even in darkness. And the grace of God's perseverance still enables the redemptive history finally to triumph over the secular one. The only secret to victory is for the saints to insist on faith in Divine Creation and Redemption. The redemptive history still exists for secular history.

c. **Christology and anthropology**

The Primeval History also introduced the Pre-incarnational Christology well. Christ, the Son of God, diversely revealed himself as follows: The Creator, the Redeemer, and the Judge. Even before His incarnation, however, all His different ministries shared the same goal of building God's Kingdom on earth.

The Primeval History also shows two kinds of anthropology: Christological and Soteriological. Soteriological anthropology speaks of humans who need the redemptive work of Coming

Christ. However, Christological anthropology says about Christ to come as the Redeemer, foretold by humane representatives: Adam and Noah.

The first man, Adam, typifies Christ, the second and last Adam to come. Seth, born instead of the dead Abel, predicted Christ, who will rose from the dead. Noah, who saved humanity through his righteous deed, foretold that the Coming Christ will redeem humankind through His righteousness. After the Flood, Noah became a new ancestor. Likewise, He will become the ancestor of the new humanity after the last judgment by fire.

c. **Soteriology**

The Old Testament already explained soteriology from the perspective of movement. The Fall expelled Adam and Eve out of the Edenic Garden. Life outside the Garden was the result of God's curse. However, the Flood's salvation brought Noah and his family from the old world into a new one. A fresh start in the renewed world was the result of Divine redemption. It is the Old-Testamental doctrine of soteriology from the concept of movement.

And the Old Testament says that soteriology depends on representative righteousness. Adam allowed his descendants to live in the Garden of Eden. However, his disobedience had thrown Adam and his descendants out of it. Noah's righteous deeds made his children redeemed and helped them become the new humanity in the renewed world after the Flood.

Representative righteousness and movement salvation were

two inseparable aspects of the old-Testamental soteriology. This soteriology did not change after Nimrod's Tower of Babel. Having chosen a person as representative among humanity, God asked him to move out of his native village to a specific place. Thus, the movement of location changed his spiritual belonging.

. others

From the personal perspective, Adam (Genesis 1-3), Seth (Gen. 4-8), and Noah (Gen. 9-11) made up the Primeval History (Genesis 1-11). But from the covenantal perspective, the Covenants of Creation (Genesis 2:17), Redemption (Genesis 3:15), and Preservation (Genesis 9:1-17) also consist of it.

The Primeval History showed several narratives. And narratives were a series of events that make up the story. The Primeval History began with the Creation and ended up with the Tower of Babel incident. In the process between them, there are events of Fall, Redemption, and Flood.

After all, Primeval History was a narrative composed of epochal historical events such as Creation, Fall, Redemption, Flood, and Tower of Babel.

The narrative was an oral Bible. The advantage of a narrative was in the form of the story. Stories were easy to tell and to remember. Simultaneously, stories encompass all kinds of contents: the universe, nature, human society, human life, and humans. They organically connect various themes within themselves. Nevertheless, A story is easy to deliver to other generations. It is why the narrative was the way of writing the Bible.

The narrative way of story-telling argues that thematic biblical interpretation is not correct. The narrative gives comprehensive teaching by organically intertwining various subjects in the historical field. Although it is a narrative, there are multiple teachings to be interpreted from the issues' perspective. It is wrong to interpret a story as only one subject.

After the Primeval History, the universal history of humanity no longer existed in the Bible. Instead, the Bible newly began the history of the chosen people. Even though the chosen people's history was as holy as the redemptive one, it would eventually be no different from the secular one.

Primeval History is the first historical record of the Bible. Start indicates what the future direction and goal will be. Besides, the Primeval History would help study how humankind's narratives and the chosen people would unfold in the future. The lessons and teachings of the Primeval History are instrumental and helpful to interpret worldly history.

The incident of the Babel Tower dramatically changed God's tactics. God called upon Abram at Ur of Chaldea. His tactical aim was to designate Abram as a patriarch of a chosen people. God commanded him to go away from his native to the land of Canaan. Why did God choose Canaan? Because the land of Canaan was very suitable for the nomadic life for the chosen people to live in the future.

Chapter 4

Canaanite Geopolitics

Geopolitics is studying the political, military, and economic impacts of the geographical environment on countries and peoples from a macro perspective. On the other hand, faith life is living in a personal relationship between God and man. God's existence and His Words are its centers, foundation, and beginning. However, God, the Creator, provides and controls nature and human society.

Like geopolitics, the Bible also records what kinds of affections on human society the relationship between time as a variable factor and space as a constant factor. As an immutable element, nature can influence human society and individual believers as variable elements.

Canaan made an abrupt appearance from the 12th chapter of Genesis and became the stage and background of the Bible until the end. Biblical interpretations require geopolitical knowledge about Canaan. The lack of understanding urges readers to generalize and interpret a biblical text by the common sense of their contemporary culture and history. It is because they don't know why God designated Canaan as the promised land.

1. **Geographical characteristics of Canaan**

Ezekiel, one of the prophets in the 7- 8th century B.C., foretold the imminent destruction of the southern Judean Dynasty. Explaining the reason and cause, he said that Israel was in the midst of the land (Ezekiel 38:12). He was familiar with the geographical characteristics of Canaan.

"**Thus saith the Lord God; This [is] Jerusalem: I have set it in the midst of the nations and countries [that are] round about her.**" (Ezeiel5:5, 6, 7, 14)

Geographically, Canaan was a land-between. It was among three continents: Europe, Asia, and Africa. Naturally, Canaan was always under constant influence from the three continents in race, culture, and religion.

Ethnically, the descendants of Shem, Ham, and Japheth lived around Canaan. Canaan was exactly among them. Culturally, Canaan was at the center of the Fertile Crescent between the birthplaces of ancient agricultural society: Mesopotamia in the north and Egypt in the south. Besides this, the Hittite Empire (18-12 centuries B.C.) was the forerunner of the Anatolian peninsula's iron-age civilization. The Phoenician, an ancient maritime trade empire, was along the eastern coast of the Mediterranean Sea. Religiously, Canaan was between both sides of the Mesopotamian and Egyptian agricultural gods.

And geologically, Canaan was along the boundary where the African and Arabian earthquake plates met each other. Earthquakes always threatened Canaanites. And climatologically, it was possible to meet all four worldly climates in Canaan: The Mediterranean climate in the west (wet wind), desert climate from the eastern Arabian Peninsula (dry, hot wind), the continental weather in the north (cold wind), and tropical climate in the south equator (hot, dry wind).

The climatical combinations determine seasonal weather in Canaan. A pair of the Mediterranean climate and desert or tropical climate invites summer without rain. Most of the plants die in summer. A couple of the Mediterranean climate and continental weather let winter with much rain come into Canaan. All plants come alive in winter. Naturally, summer in Canaan is like winter in other continents, while winter in Canaan - like spring reviving all things as in other countries. It is why biblical climatical expressions and explanations are different from those of other continents and countries.

2. Geopolitical characteristics of Canaan

Geopolitically, Canaan served as a land bridge connecting the continents of Africa, Europe, and Asia. It also played an unfortunate role as a buffer zone among them. It was why Canaan had been severely affected easily, openly exposing itself to the outside.

The bridging role had advantages and disadvantages at the same time. It gave opportunities for cultural development and growth. At the same time, it could kill cultural identity in reverse. There were other benefits too. Strong Canaan could easily give good influence around itself.

However, the buffering role was always negative. Whenever a new empire appeared in the south or north, a sudden whirlwind of war caught Canaan. The great powers tried to expand the kingdom's territory and advance to the other continent through Canaan. International wars frequently erupted in Megiddo on the Jezreel Plain, the most grained region of Canaan.

And geological and meteorological conditions influenced the quality of Canaanitic life. Frequent earthquakes threatened settled life, and the changing weather and climate made life hard and challenging. Geological and meteorological factors remained unchanged even though there happened changes and differences in race, history, and culture.

Canaanitic life was training itself. Canaanites, born and raised in Canaan, could adapt themselves well to any other place at any time. God well knew Canaan from the perspectives of geopolitics and geology. Intentionally and deliberately, God called Abram from Ur of Chaldea, saying to him:

"Now the LORD had said unto Abram, Get thee out of thy country, and from thy kindred, and from thy father's house, unto a land that I will shew thee: And I will make of thee a great nation, and I will bless thee, and make thy name great; and thou shalt be a blessing: And I will bless them that bless thee, and curse him that curseth thee: and in thee shall all families of the earth be blessed." (Genesis12:1-3)

3.   Canaan, the Promised Land

Canaan was not a land flowing with milk and honey. Canaanites always had to live under invasions and attacks from neighboring countries. Life conditions were usually unstable. Paradoxically, the Bible records 20 times Canaan as a land of blessings flowing with milk and honey. The prophet Ezekiel specially introduced Canaan as the glory of all lands (Ezekiel 20:6, 15).

"And I am come down to deliver them out of the hand of the Egyptians, and to bring them up out of that land unto a good land and a large, unto a land flowing with milk and honey; unto the place of the Canaanites, and the Hittites, and the Amorites, and the Perizzites, and the Hivites, and the Jebusites."(Exodus3:8)

God, who called Moses on Mount Sinai, revealed Canaan as a land of blessings flowing with milk and honey. However, the natives were already living there. Later, Moses also introduced Canaan on the plains of Moab as follows:

"For the land, whither thou goest in to possess it, [is] not as the land of Egypt, from whence ye came out, where thou sowedst thy seed, and wateredst [it] with thy foot, as a garden of herbs: But the land, whither ye go to possess it, [is] a land of hills and valleys, [and] drinketh water of the rain of heaven: A land which the LORD thy God careth for: the eyes of the LORD thy God [are] always upon it, from the beginning of the year even unto the end of the year. And it shall come to pass, if ye shall hearken diligently unto my commandments which I command you this day, to love the

LORD your God, and to serve him with all your heart and with all your soul, That I will give [you] the rain of your land in his due season, the first rain and the latter rain, that thou mayest gather in thy corn, and thy wine, and thine oil. And I will send grass in thy fields for thy cattle, that thou mayest eat and be full."(Deut.11:10-15)

Unlike Egypt and Mesopotamia, Canaan was a land of mountains and valleys without a vast plain for agriculture. Farming there was not possible only with human efforts. A good harvest came only when the sky rained in time. Knowing this well, Moses revealed the secret to make Canaan a land flowing with milk and honey.

In Canaan, Israel would have to obey the law earnestly. As commanded by the law, Israel must have driven all the Gentiles out of Canaan. However, when Israel, wanting to flourish together with the natives, did not follow the law, they would have harmed themselves.

"But if ye will not drive out the inhabitants of the land from before you; then it shall come to pass, that those which ye let remain of them [shall be] pricks in your eyes, and thorns in your sides, and shall vex you in the land wherein ye dwell"(Num.33:55)

"Wherefore I also said, I will not drive them out from before you, but they shall be [as thorns] in your sides, and their gods shall be a snare unto you."(Judges2:3)

To conquer Canaan, Israel would have to fight the seven native tribes. The natives of Canaan lived an agricultural life, while Israel, the chosen people, would live a nomadic life. In the aspects of religion and ideology, these two lifestyles would not meet altogether with each other. Coexistence would be impossible. There would remain only one question which one would eat up the other.

First, Israel would have to conquer Canaan's natives, and next, continue to fight against their corrupt customs of agricultural life. For this test, God would not deliberately destroy most of them. Therefore, only the law's observance will lead Israel to build up a kingdom of perfect blessing in the poor Canaan.

Canaanitic geopolitics reveals another fact. The wilderness of southern Negeb occupies 52% of Canaan. The annual rainfall here is less than 150 mm. Canaan was famous for the land with mountains and valleys and also with a wasteland. In the days of the Old Testament, Israel had to live a nomadic life inevitably.

There was agricultural land in the remaining 48% of Canaan. Hula Valley in northern Galilee, the Plains of Jezreel, the coastal plains of Akko, Sharon, Philistine, and the Jordan River where alluvial soils piled up. The annual rainfall of those regions exceeds 600 mm. These areas were perfect agricultural land. However, strong natives had already settled there. The patriarch and Israel had no choice but to live nomadic lives in the wilderness (Gen. 47:3).

Knowing this well, God deliberately chose Canaan as Israel's inheritance. Unlike the Gentiles in Canaan, the chosen people lived a different life in the Promised Land. Furthermore, the Canaanites, living agricultural life, were corrupt spiritually and ethically. The chosen people of Israel would live a holy life apart from them.

"Take heed to thyself, lest thou make a covenant with the inhabitants of the land whither thou goest, lest it be for a snare in the midst of thee: But ye shall destroy their altars, break their images, and cut down their groves: For thou shalt worship no other god: for the LORD, whose name [is] Jealous, [is] a jealous God: Lest thou make a covenant with the inhabitants of the land, and they go a whoring after their gods, and do sacrifice unto their gods, and [one] call thee, and thou eat of his sacrifice; And thou take of their daughters unto thy sons, and their daughters go a whoring after their gods, and make thy sons go a whoring after their gods. Thou shalt make thee no molten gods." (Exodus34:12-17)

Before and after the Flood, the descendants of Adam and Noah lived corrupt agricultural life. In that society, people regarded God and nature as the objects of human conquest. The ruler became a divine being to possess absolute power. This kind of community usually became totalitarian and authoritarian. It was because agricultural society denied the faith in God, the Creator.

God had to establish His Kingdom different from the corrupt agricultural society in Canaan. Canaanitic geopolitics was well suitable for God's purpose. Because it was a less-developed area, far from the farming civilizations of the world, yet its location was in the center of the world. From here, the faith in Divine Creation would go abroad to the world through the chosen people.

Agricultural life always pursues material prosperity and economic wealth from the land. However, nomadic life sees the earth as a temporary place to stay to obtain grass. Nomadic life, unlike agricultural one, does not cling to space. And Israel, as a nomad, served only One God, the Creator. However, surrounding gentiles, as farmers, served Baal, an agricultural god. The faith in Jehovah was a heavenly religion, while the belief in Baal - an earthly religion to satisfy human greed.

The inter-ethnic battles between Israel and the Gentiles were like a religious war between Jehovah and Baal, and like an ideological struggle between different ideas, philosophies, and values. How did Israel win?

Israeli adherence to nomadic life would help easily win against the Gentiles. Nomad usually lives hard to survive in the wilderness. Life itself is training and discipline. In war, nomads are excellent fighters as horsemen, while farmers - untrained infantry living peacefully in cities. Nomads are superior to farmers.

And nomadic life would help Israel continue to obey God, the Creator, to distinguish themselves from the Gentile farmers. Keeping religious and cultural identity was the secret to victory in warfare, spiritual and ideological.

4.   **God's Kingdom in Canaan**

To survive in Canaan, the patriarch and Israel had to do three opposite things. First, they had to escape from a prosperous agricultural society. And next, they had to found a nomadic community in Canaan. Afterward, they had to continue the religious and ideological struggles with the natives living in agricultural life. Canaanite geopolitics also explains this well.

Canaan was far from Egypt and Mesopotamia, where agricultural culture flourished. However, Canaan plays the roles of bridge and buffer zone between them. Their cultural influence was inevitable. However, the geopolitical characteristics – a land of mountains and valleys - alleviated the impact from outside. On the one hand, Canaan was open, but on the other hand, closed.

The problem was that inside Canaan remained the natives living in agricultural life. Natives had already settled in the agricultural plains. On the other hand, Israel had to live a nomadic life, mainly in the mountains, valleys, and wilderness. But they, as semi-nomads, lived around the village and exchanged products with farmers. Israel lived not in the center but the vicinity. It was because Israel, as a nomad, had to be distinguished from farmers while in contact with agricultural society.

Canaan was not a symbol of the heavenly kingdom to enter through bodily death. Canaan, the promised land, was a geopolitical part of the world. Israel would have to build the Kingdom of God, where the Mosaic Law should rule. Israel would be utterly different from the gentile countries inside and around it. Even the kings of Israel should obey the law. Israel would realize a full sense of rule by Mosaic law in Canaan.

In those days, the gentile kings, as an extraterritorial entity, were an authoritarian ruler. The people of the agricultural society were slaves living under rule by the king's virtues. In comparison with Israel, the gentile countries did not guarantee social freedom and equality.

The ruler of nomadic society is like a shepherd (2 Sam. 5:2). Shepherds are sacrificing servers who find grass, water, and rest and lead sheep there. The land providing these three belongs to the public, not to the private. And the land is just one of the places where shepherds live for a while, depending on the season. Naturally, neighbors are brothers and colleagues in nomadic society. Geopolitical Canaan helped Israel well live this nomadic life.

In Canaan, Israel would be the most advanced country as the Kingdom of God. Using geopolitical strengths as a bridge and buffer zone, he could propagate to neighboring gentile countries and peoples that Jehovah, the God of Israel, was the only God in the world. It was a holy mission to carry out in Canaan after the Exodus of Israel from Egypt.

Canaanite geopolitics also helped Israel carry out the mission effectively. Canaan was open outwards but closed inwards. Canaan, as a land of mountains, valleys, and wasteland, was among the world. For example, the Judean wilderness rounds the city of Jerusalem, which quickly leads to the outside world. The nomadic life helped Israel to preserve the creative faith and to continue an eschatological life dominated by time, not space.

The kingdom of David was the historical realization of God's kingdom to be built up in Canaan. The Davidic dynasty showed the climax of the Divine rule by Mosaic law. The law did not allow even the king or the nobles to remove their neighbor's landmark.

Economically, the landmark meant the fundamental living right in Canaan, the promised land. Politically, it was a token of Israel's citizenship. And religiously, it was a sign of God's redemption by the Exodus event.

In a gentile country, there was no landmark system, and all land belonged to the property of the king and nobles. This fact testified that the Kingdom of David was a state which ultimately realized the rule by law in Canaan three thousand years ago. It showed the state of the best-developed country today. Only the faith in Divine creation made it possible.

However, the Davidic dynasty symbolized God's kingdom to be set up by the Coming Messiah. The prototype will come only when the type withdraws. Northern Israel and southern Judah were destroyed by Assyria and Babylon, respectively. It was because Israel and Judah were absorbed into the agricultural society and religiously joined Baal worship.

Abandoning the nomadic life came to deny the faith in Divine creation and caused the chosen people to lose their holiness. Along with this also disappeared the geopolitical meanings and teachings of Canaan. After the destruction of Israel and Judah, God's kingdom, as shown in the New Testament, became an intangible reality, unlike the Old Testament. Canaan's geopolitical meaning was changed into the abstract one and converted the Old Testament's earthly aspect into the heavenly one of the New Testament.

5. New Testamental Kingdom of God

The inter-Testamental history covers about 400 years between Malachi's book, the last book of the Old Testament, and the Gospel of Mathew, the first book of the New Testament. During this time, Rabbinical Judaism was in its heyday. The rabbis from the Pharisees religiously ruled the Jews. But Judaism had already deviated from the Pentateuch.

The Jews returned from Babylonian captivity in the 6th century B.C. and rebuilt the Zerubbabel Temple. However, they had already fallen so spiritually that the prophet Malachi lamented, saying:

"Who [is there] even among you that would shut the doors [for nought]? neither do ye kindle [fire] on mine altar for nought. I have no pleasure in you, saith the LORD of hosts, neither will I accept an offering at your hand."(Mal.1:10)

In 164 B.C., Antiochus Epiphanius IV (175-163 B.C.) of the Syrian Seleucid dynasty severely suppressed Judaism, prohibiting circumcision, Sabbath, and observance of the law. He built a statue of Zeus in the Temple and offered a pig's head as a sacrifice. He completely defiled the Temple of Zerubbabel.

Then, the Maccabi Revolution broke out, and later, the Hasmonean, the Jewish independence dynasty, was founded. In 64 B.C., Roman General Pompeii destroyed the dynasty. Herod the great, governor of Judea by the Roman regime, rebuilt and expanded the Zerubbabel Temple in 20 B.C. Herod from Idumea, converted to Judaism, built the Second Temple more massive and more monumental than the Solomon Temple to achieve his political purposes.

When the Roman Empire controlled the land of Canaan, Jesus was born in the 3rd year B.C. He had lived His private life for 30 years and His official life for three years. For about 30 years, Jesus had visited the Temple not less than 50 times. Jesus said of Judaism later as follows:

"I am come in my Father's name, and ye receive me not: if another shall come in his own name, him ye will receive. How can ye believe, which receive honour one of another, and seek not the honour that [cometh] from God only? Do not think that I will accuse you to the Father: there is [one] that accuseth you, [even] Moses, in whom ye trust. For had ye believed Moses, ye would have believed me: for he wrote of me. But if ye believe not his writings, how shall ye believe my words?" (John5:43-47)

The Jews were irrelevant to Moses in the Old Testament

and were spiritually stubborn as the prophet Isaiah foretold (Isaiah 6:8-13). The nationalism of Rabbinic Judaism did not fit into the New Testament era that transcended the bloody lineage. Jesus had a keen interest not in rebuilding the Davidic dynasty but in building the Kingdom of God. It was contrary to Jewish expectations.

He was born as a king (Luke 1:31-33). As an official king, however, He had not lived among His people for 30 years. The baptism of John the Baptist inaugurated Him as the Messiah. Immediately after winning the wilderness test, he proclaimed that God's kingdom was at hand (Mark 1:9-15). In the middle of His public life, he told the parables of heaven and revealed its secret: the low beginning, modest growth, and the sharp end of the kingdom of God (Matthew 13). At the end of his public life, He told the parables of heaven again, revealing the linkage of His death, resurrection, ascension, and second coming with the growth and glorious completion of God's kingdom (Matthew 25). And for 40 days after the resurrection, Jesus taught the disciples the things of the kingdom (Acts 1:3).

He never officially revealed Himself as king before and after his resurrection. His kingdom was a spiritual reality as an invisible entity, unlike that of the Old Testament. God's kingdom transcends space. At His second coming, the Divine Kingdom will finally reveal its splendor.

After the resurrection, He became the Lord of lords (Acts 2:36). His kingdom could not remain limited to the space of Canaan and the bloody lineage of Jews. And He now rules His people by His words and the Holy Spirit. Thus, His rule overcomes space, distance, and time. Whosoever believes in Jesus as the Redeemer may enter His kingdom.

"**Jesus answered and said unto him, Verily, verily, I say unto thee, Except a man be born again, he cannot see the kingdom of God. Nicodemus saith unto him, How can a man be born when he is old? Can he enter the second time into his mother's womb, and be born? Jesus answered, Verily, verily, I say unto thee, Except a man be born of water and [of] the Spirit, he cannot enter into the kingdom of God.**"(John3:3-5)

The Old Testament, using earthly type and symbol, predicted the heavenly prototype of the New Testament. The archetype does not depend on flesh and ground elements. Despite the differences, Canaanitic geopolitics of the Old Testament have theological meanings to explain the kingdom of God of the New Testament era.

In the times of the Old Testament, Canaan was the world where Israel lived. In New Testament times, Canaan belonged to the Roman Empire occupying Europe, Africa, and Asia. Thanks to the Roman Empires, the kingdom of God also surpassed the geopolitical Canaan. Thus, the church and the saints were able to cross the border of Canaan freely.

Interestingly enough, Canaan's geopolitics testifies that the kingdom of God, the church, and the saints are no different from Israel in the Old Testament. Israel became God's people physically, while new Israel becomes God's people spiritually.

Despite the difference between spirit and body, they are the same in that they are God's people.

Israel of the Old-Testament did three conflicting things. Israel escaped from Egypt's agricultural society. They conquered Canaan to establish a nomadic community. And to protect the nomadic culture, they were always on an alert against the inner agrarian culture.

Israel of the New Testament also has to do the same thing spiritually. They do not need to move from place to place like the Old Testament Israel. Surprisingly enough, the redemption of the New Testament makes spiritual movement possible.

"Who hath delivered us from the power of darkness, and hath translated [us] into the kingdom of his dear Son. In whom we have redemption through his blood, [even] the forgiveness of sins:" (Col.1:13-14)

The kingdom of God, into which the redeemed saints enter, is in the world like Canaan. They have to wage two types of fights: Outward struggle against the world and inward battle inside the church.

"Finally, my brethren, be strong in the Lord, and in the power of his might. Put on the whole armour of God, that ye may be able to stand against the wiles of the devil. For we wrestle not against flesh and blood, but against principalities, against powers, against the rulers of the darkness of this world, against spiritual wickedness in high

[places]." (Ephes.6:10-12)

"**If so be that ye have heard him, and have been taught by him, as the truth is in Jesus: That ye put off concerning the former conversation the old man, which is corrupt according to the deceitful lusts; And be renewed in the spirit of your mind; And that ye put on the new man, which after God is created in righteousness and true holiness.**" (Ephes.4:21-24)

The redemption through Exodus made Israel physically live in Canaan, the promised land. Likewise, the redemption through Jesus's death and resurrection makes saints spiritually live in Canaan. It means that the New-Testamental saints can learn the geopolitical teachings of Canaan as theological lessons.

And Canaan in Old Testament times served as a bridge and buffer zone. It means that Israel lived in the center of the world. It is appliable to God's kingdom, the church, and the saints of the New-Testamental era. The saints have two contradicting efforts.

The world easily influences on saints and sometimes attacks them. It means that they have to protect themselves spiritually from the world. On the other hand, they can easily preach the Gospel to the world. It means that they must have open relationships with the world. Openness and closeness are necessary for saints' spiritual survival.

Besides, they live their eschatological life on the temporal way of thinking and differentiate themselves from people who live a hedonic life on the spatial way of thinking. They preach and inform by lifestyle the Gospel of Jesus Christ to the world. It also requires both the openness and closeness of the saints.

And frequent earthquakes threatened Canaanites, and ever-changing weather and climate always badly influenced their life. Likewise, the saints of the New Testament still feel uneasy in a Canaan-like world. The faith confession in Jesus Christ as Redeemer pushes them to meet adversity and tribulation. On the other hand, they, keeping the faith, have to adapt to the world's changes and trends.

Israel, the chosen people, was a kingdom of priests. Living in Canaan was like living in the center of the world. Israel had no guarantee to live in prosperity and wealth as long as they lived in Canaan. The same goes well with the saints of the New Testament. Jesus taught that saints have to play the role of salt and light of the world, to lighten a town under the mountain (Matthew 5:13-16). This role always requires self-sacrifice.

The only way to survive is for the saints to carry out their mission. They have to shed light upon the darkness of the world and, at the same time, keeping the taste of salt to prevent the corruption of the world. Otherwise, the dark buries the light, and tasteless salt is cast out and trodden under the foot of men.

"Ye are the salt of the earth: but if the salt have lost his savour, wherewith shall it be salted? it is thenceforth good for nothing, but to be cast out, and to be trodden under foot of men. Ye are the light of the world. A city that is set on an hill cannot be hid. Neither do men light a candle, and put it under a bushel, but on a candlestick; and it giveth light unto all that are in the house. Let your light so shine before men, that they may see your good works, and glorify your Father which is in heaven." (Math.5:13-16)

In Old Testament times, Israel waged war in the blood and flesh. However, in New Testament times, saints wage spiritual warfare with the power of darkness belonging to Satan. They, belonging to the heavenly kingdom, have to serve the world as citizens of the earthly realm. Then, they can play the roles of light and salt of the world.

To play an outstanding role, saints have to take double attitudes toward the world. Canaan's geopolitics taught that the world was not always favorable to the saints. And the nomadic life was radically different from the agricultural one. Therefore, Old Testamental patriarchs, like semi-nomads, lived near villages but not in its center. Saints also need this nomadic life of faith even in the New-Testamental age.

The apostle Paul already said about this.

"But this I say, brethren, the time [is] short: it remaineth, that both they that have wives be as though they had none; And they that weep, as though they wept not; and they that rejoice, as though they rejoiced not; and they that buy, as though they possessed not; And they that use this world, as not abusing [it]: for the fashion of this world passeth away."(1Co7:29-31)

Jesus also advised His disciples to live the nomadic life of faith.

"Lay not up for yourselves treasures upon earth, where moth and rust doth corrupt, and where thieves break through and steal: But lay up for yourselves treasures in heaven, where neither moth nor rust doth corrupt, and where thieves do not break through nor steal: For where your treasure is, there will your heart be also. The light of the body is the eye: if therefore thine eye be single, thy whole body shall be full of light. But if thine eye be evil, thy whole body shall be full of darkness. If therefore the light that is in thee be darkness, how great [is] that darkness! No man can serve two masters: for either he will hate the one, and love the other; or else he will hold to the one, and despise the other. Ye cannot serve God and mammon."(Math.6:19-24)

Saints are citizens of the earthly kingdom, as well as those of the heavenly kingdom. They, living in the world, must be distinguished from the world. There is a biblical warning about it.

"Yet I had planted thee a noble vine, wholly a right seed: how then art thou turned into the degenerate plant of a strange vine unto me?"(Jerem.2:21)

"And the word of the LORD came unto me, saying, Son of man, What is the vine tree more than any tree, [or than] a branch which is among the trees of the forest? Shall wood be taken thereof to do any work? or will [men] take a pin of it to hang any vessel thereon? Behold, it is cast into the fire for fuel; the fire devoureth both the ends of it, and the midst of it is burned. Is it meet for [any] work?" (Esk.15:1-4)

"I am the vine, ye [are] the branches: He that abideth in me, and I in him, the same bringeth forth much fruit: for without me ye can do nothing. If a man abide not in me, he is cast forth as a branch, and is withered; and men gather them, and cast [them] into the fire, and they are burned. If ye abide in me, and my words abide in you, ye shall ask what ye will, and it shall be done unto you. Herein is my Father glorified, that ye bear much fruit; so shall ye be my disciples." (John15:5-8)

Saints, redeemed for Divine mission, must know the world. However, they must not absorb themselves into the world. As citizens of the world, saints can be active in politics, economy, culture, and society. But they cannot be with anything which forcedly demands the agricultural way of thinking. Sometimes the saints have to do social alienation or isolation voluntarily. It is because the redeemed saints of the New Testament are spiritual nomads.

Like Israel, saints of the New Testament always expose themselves to the test of living a nomadic way of life. This test has two purposes: tempting the abandoned to ruin and training the chosen to heighten the sanctification level. It is why saints should always be on guard against worldly thoughts, philosophy, and ideas based on agricultural society or atheism.

Jesus's Redemption changed the Old Testament's earthly aspect into the heavenly one of the New Testament. There remains the nomadic life of faith, even in the age of the Gospel of Heaven.

6.   **Canaan, deserted land**

In A.D. 70, the Roman Empire destroyed the Temple of Jerusalem. Before the destruction, the Jewish members of the early church had already left Jerusalem. And in 136 A.D., the Second Jewish Revolt by Bar Kokhba no longer allowed Jews to stay in Jerusalem. The Roman Empire officially renamed Canaan   Palestine. And the cities and towns became quickly Romanized. Canaan utterly converted itself into a land of Gentiles.

Interestingly enough, in the last 2,000 years, Canaan had been dominated by European Christianity for only 500 years: For 300 years by the Byzantine Empire and 200 years by the Crusades. For the remaining 1,500 years, the Roman Empire had occupied it for about 300 years and Muslims - for 1,200 years. Thus, Canaan has been entirely far away from the Bible for a long time.

Christianity grew and developed in Europe. For 1,500 years,

the prolonged occupation of Canaan by Muslims had not allowed European Christianity to advance eastward. Europeans had made attempts to turn west. The efforts enabled them to discover a new continent in the 15th century. The Christian Gospel continued to advance westward. During this period, Christianity entirely forgot about the biblical land of Canaan as well as its geopolitics.

From the 2nd century, Church Fathers began to assert an alternative theology that Gentiles replaced Jews. And Christianity developed in Europe, which was dominated by Roman Greek culture. The Church Fathers knew Plato and Aristoteles better than Moses. Accordingly, they abandoned the theological, philosophical, and sociological teachings from Canaanitic geopolitics.

Regardless of Canaan's geopolitics, the Fathers had interpreted the biblical texts. Systematic theology developed a thematic interpretation of the Bible. Biblical books were generalized by common sense, exclusive of history and culture.

Gradually, Christianity became one of the worldly religions. Christian theology also fell into a specialized study. Western Christianity again repeated the faults committed by Judaism. The oral tradition of Judaism has nothing to do with the Pentateuch. Likewise, Christian theology has nothing to do with the Bible.

Canaanitic geopolitics testify that even in the New Testament era, the kingdom of God, the church, and the saints are in the midst of a hostile world. European churches forgot this. Northern Israel and southern Judah gradually joined the surrounding agricultural culture, so their society became corrupt and obscene like a gentile society. God destroyed them by judgment.

Likewise, Christianity of the New Testament era should have known that the world was hostile but failed. Since the Byzantine Empire recognized Christianity as the state religion, the world had been no longer an enemy of the church. European Christianity became more and more Greek. The dualistic way of interpretation abandoned much of the biblical teachings.

The negligence of The Creation article (Genesis 1-2) and Canaanitic geopolitics causes Christianity to lose the direction and goal of biblical interpretation. The church and saints can serve as a lightening city on the mountain when retrieving the Divine Creation and Canaanitic geopolitics' theological meaning.

The better the city lights at the top of the hill, the more the town below the mountain can be in enlightenment. A church and a saint are like an upper village, while the world – a lower village.

"Ye are the light of the world. A city that is set on an hill cannot be hid. Neither do men light a candle, and put it under a bushel, but on a candlestick; and it giveth light unto all that are in the house. Let your light so shine before men, that they may see your good works, and glorify your Father which is in heaven."(Math5:14-16)

Christianity does not know that the nomadic culture is the

dominant one of the Bible and interprets the Bible with agricultural civilization's glasses. Today, Christianity has become a syncretistic religion. Nowadays, the Catholic, representing Greek Christianity, already abandoned the exclusiveness and specialty of the Bible and is trying to join other faiths.

It is necessary to reinterpret the Bible with the glasses of nomadic culture. Then, the restored confidence in biblical Creation and Redemption will make Christianity re-born as the religion of salvation.

7. Abraham's leaving for Canaan

God called up Abram and commanded him to go to the land he would show (Genesis 12:1). Abram did not know where to go, but he obeyed in faith. His faith came from hearing the word of God (Rom. 10:17). At that time, the oral Bible was Primitive History (Genesis 1-11). The History helped him to be justified by faith. It was essential to that extent.

Geopolitically, Canaan was a place amid the world and suitable for nomadic life. Abram's descendants would establish God's Kingdom based on nomadic culture there. And God called upon Abram from Ur of Chaldea. But God would direct and lead him to Canaan. The distance between them was nearly 3,000 kilometers. Even Abram could not have quickly obeyed.

Farmers couldn't travel that long distances from Chaldea Ur to Canaan. They had to move at least six months. They could not procure lots of road foods for the family. However, Abram was a nomadic descendant of Shem. Nomads were adept at moving. Abram would be able to travel long distances, leading a nomadic life on the way.

Canaan was far from Egypt and Mesopotamia, where farming culture was very corrupted. Canaan was an outsider in the agricultural culture. As a would-be ancestor of the chosen people, Abram had to escape from the agrarian culture and move to Canaan. Like Adam of Primitive History, Abram would live in Canaan like Adam of the chosen people's history. The redemptive history of the chosen people would replace Primitive History and newly restart.

Christ, the Son of God, called Abram from Chaldea Ur. Even before incarnation, as God the Creator, He would work anew in the chosen people's history. The same Deity was the Lord of the Primeval History and would be the Lord of the chosen people's history. The chosen people's redemptive history would not be different from Primitive History in their direction and goal.

8. Canaan in the biblical meaning

Canaan, the promised land, was well suited to a nomadic society, but not to an agricultural community. It was a barren area, where you could not live without giving rain in time from the sky. And Lord always kept eyes Canaan from the beginning of the year to the end, caring for it. It was Canaan's land, explained in the book of Deuteronomy of the Old Testament (11:10-12ct.).

Ancient Egypt boasted an incredible agricultural culture. There you could live as well as you made efforts with human wisdom and power. Egyptians did not need God's grace or help at all. Spiritually Egypt was like a cursed land. Canaan, on the other hand, was not like Egypt. People could not live there without God. They had to depend upon God's grace every day. In this respect, Canaan was like a blessed land to Israel.

Then, what is the difference between agricultural and nomadic societies? Nomadic society is not settled, unlike agrarian society. Nomads live in wilderness places. They are very sensitive to seasonal changes to find grass and move in time. They do not so much cling to the area and space.

They own properties only to the extent that they might move comfortably and efficiently. Cattles is as precious as their life, and labor is so scarce and limited in the wilderness. Nomads live by helping one another. Nomadic society, therefore, is politically democratic. Agricultural society, on the other hand, is totalitarian.

Nomadic society, unlike farming society, is mostly governed by the concept of time. If you miss the time and period of movement, you lose everything. Nomads have to move along the direction, indicated by the seasonal change of time. And, unlike farmers, nomads very well know about human incompetence, seeing the grandeur of nature. They live in compliance with natural circumstances. Nomadic society religiously does not worship material images and powers as idols.

From the biblical view of points, the believer's way of life is closer to a non-settling nomadic society than to a settled agricultural community. God calls his chosen ones out of the farming culture to lead into a nomadic one. The event of Exodus is a good example. It is spiritually the same with the experience of N.T time.

By the grace of redemption, sinners become citizens of the kingdom of God. They have to live new entities in philosophy, ideas, and systems of values, which are entirely different from this world. Those of the Heavenly kingdom replace those of the earthly realm. In the New Testament times, believers carry out spiritual warfare every day to set up and expand God's kingdom in this world.

Chapter 5

Conclusion

Structurally, the Bible can be analyzed as follows:

	Divine Decrees	Primeval History	Chosen History	Humanity history
Bible	Eph.1:4-6	Genesis 1-11	Genesis12-Mal.	Mathew. - Rev.
meaning	Plan	start	development	fulfillment
humankind	Universal	universal	Limited	Limited universal
ancestor	Christ	Adam	Abraham	Christ
history	Eternal Decrees	Secular	Redemptive	secular
goal	God's Family	God's Kingdom		

The Eternal Decrees was like a Plan set up by God before the creation of the world. God, the Planner, would achieve the Project's purpose in time determined by Him. The set timetable logically prepared the Plan. Its logical order also decided the times to do the planned things. After all, the logic of the Eternal Decrees was also subject to time.

Thus, Primeval History (Genesis 1-11), as Bible's first record, also followed the Eternal Decree's schedule. God the Father set up the Decrees before the Creation, and God the Son historically realized it after the Creation. Therefore, the Creation, the first event of the Primeval History, was also subject to time. It was already eschatological.

The Biblical Creation also showed how God the Father would work to build God's kingdom as His Decrees' ultimate goal. In other words, the Primeval History as secular history was the history of God's Kingdom. Naturally, the Primeval History was subject to God's set time. In other words, it was also eschatological.

The Primeval History reveals how the universal history of humanity began. It is also the superiority of the Christian Bible. The universal history tells that God, the Creator, naturally transcends the bloody lineage.

Jehovah cannot be the only Jewish national god. Therefore, a Jewish consciousness of the chosen people is not right in the New Testament times. An alternative theology is also not biblical. It is wrong that this theology excludes Jews. Jesus Christ is the Savior of all peoples, including the Jews.

The Primeval History testifies that the created became the fallen and lost any reason and purpose to exist before God. Instantly after the Fall, God promised redemption for the fallen. Until reaching the Divine goal of Creation, God had to love even the lost (John 3:16) continually. The Chosen people's history, following the Primeval History, was no exception.

The Son's future Redemption would also aim to achieve Father's Decrees and Creation's purpose, already set by schedule. The Redemption would be subject to time like the Creation. The fallen would become redeemed and stand before

God as the re-created. Only the re-created would receive God's call to work again for Him.

On the other hand, Satan still worked is to cause humankind to deny God the Creator. And he always tempted humanity to enjoy only the present world, aiming to forget the Divine Redemption and eschatological aspects. As a result, human society made every effort to live a present life with ideas, philosophy, and values based on atheism.

Creation theology determined the content and character of humane sociology. They could not separate themselves from each other. Therefore, humanity always spiritually divides themselves into two groups; Creation faith and atheism. Both humans always quarrel and struggle with each other theologically and ideologically.

The Primeval History of the Bible testifies to it very well. And there was no exception in the history of the Chosen peoples after the Primeval History. The first history was also an extension of the latter.

What would be the failure of the first and second histories? It lay in abandoning the eschatological life by having denied the faith in the Creation. In other words, both of them chose thinking by visible space more than thinking by the time set by invisible God.

As a result, atheistic humankind loves His creatures more than the Creator Himself. Creature love develops into creature worship. However, it is impossible to serve or worship both of them simultaneously (Mathew6;24).

The Primeval History also records how these two kinds of histories unfolded into spiritual and ideological battles. An excellent example was the struggle between the nomadic and agricultural communities in ancient human civilization. The nomadic culture led to a time-oriented life, whereas the farming culture - to a space-oriented life.

there remain the following differences between the lives of farming and shepherding:

Inhabitation

	farming	Shepherding
work	cultivating land	Grassy field
way	Settled	Unsettled
village	city	Plain
living	castle	Tent

Survival

	farming	shepherding
Wealth source	land	Cattle
wealth	Surplus fruits	Cattle
Ownership	occupying	Sharing
How much	limitless	Limited
Who	farmer	Shepherd
military	infantries	Horsemen

Humans with creative faith chose nomadic life, while

humans with atheism - agricultural life. Biblical Primeval History testifies well how the conflict between them occurred and developed in many social fields. Every battle upgraded its level: Cain and Abel (Genesis 4) struggled individually, whereas Cain's sons fought Seth's sons (Gen. 4-5). Between the sons of God and the daughters of men (Gen. 6) happened cultural and spiritual battles. And Nimdod and Eber fought each other in a political and religious war, including their descendants.

Society

	farming	**Shepherding**
thought	Space-oriented	Time-oriented
nature	conquest	Acceptance
guider	reason/map	Faith/compass
social	vertical/subject	horizontal/equal
living	efficiency/acting	values/thinking
ethics	selfish	Sacrificing

Politics

	farming	**Shepherding**
basis	Grace/kingship	Covenant/fellowship
rulership	dictatorship	Servantship
king	ruler	Shepherd
rule	By virtues	By law
system	Authoritarianism	Democracy
Political	totalitarian	Democratic

In the Primeval History the conflicts between the two were mainly social and cultural. However, in the following history of chosen people, spiritual battles happened repeatedly between Jehovah, the creator, and Baal, the agricultural deity.

Religion

	farming	shepherding
god	Baal	Jehovah
religion	Natural deities	Creator
idolatry	Allowed	Prohibited
temple	Stationary/building	portable/tent
offering	Farming products	Cattle
history	secular	Redemptive

When the fullness of the eschatological time came, God the Son, the Creator, came down as Redeemer. His redemptive work would historically fulfill all Old-Testamental prophecies and promises. The achievement will be enjoyed only by the elect among the universal humanity. However, the fulfilled kingdom of God will reach its consummation in the coming future.

Until this time, God's Kingdom will be invisible. Like the Old Testamental believers, the New Testamental saints have to continually live a life of eschatological faith. The failure in this test will lose the chance to inherit the consummated Kingdom of God, as evidenced by the Primeval History.

Jehovah, the God of the covenant, was compared with a shepherd for Israel in the Old Testament era (Psalm 23), and the Israeli ruler was also called a shepherd (2 Sam. 5:2). Thus, shepherding culture was very different from farming culture in the political system.

Jesus Christ, who came as the Redeemer, completely restored the relationship between God and His people by His redemptive work. As a result, He became the true Shepherd, and the redeemed became His sheep (John 10:1-18). He became the true King of New Israel in New Testament times.

Thus, a saint's life of faith becomes not dependent on visible facts and phenomena. It is the accurate picture, character, and content of an adult religious life. The comparison between atheism and creative faith is as follows:

Personal life

	Atheism	Creative faith
religion	Power/wealth	Christ
orientation	Present life	After-life
philosophy	Space-oriented	Time-oriented
Thinking	reason/map	faith/compass
wealth	upon earth	in heaven
Living1	In prosperity	Daily bread
Living2	Efficiency/doing	Values/being
Ethics	selfish	Sacrificing

Social life

	Atheism	Creative faith
status	vertical/subordinate	horizontal/equal
way	Totalitarian	Personal
rule	power/by virtues	contract/by law

system	authoritarian	Democracy
life	Doing without rest	Doing with rest

Today leftist socialism represents atheistic ideas, philosophy, and values. Before the Fall, God the Creator, having allowed Satan's existence in Eden, openly tolerated atheism to work in human society.

It was why dualism is now dominating the world. Atheists regard Satan, the archenemy of God, the Creator, like a god on par with Him. Before the Fall, therefore, the Creation article already foretold that one human would break down into two.

Christian theology, influenced by Greek philosophy, ignored the material world and neglected to think out biblical ideas, philosophy, and values, based on Creationism. It resulted in Christianity's impact on faith life's religious aspect, but not on its cultural part.

What saints had to do was to live a church-centered life to complete a life of faith. It was the unfortunate result of ignoring the teachings and lessons from Creative narrative and Primeval History telling that spirits always embody itself in ideas, philosophies, and systems of various values.

Only the restoration of the Creative faith would bring back Christian thoughts, philosophy, and values automatically. This effort would be a real religious reformation.

Agricultural culture and nomadic culture are two different kinds of human civilization. The Christian Bible also records both cultures. The Creation article introduced agrarian culture from the beginning (Genesis 1:28-30, 2:15). Earth-born humanity continually depends on the products of the earth. Human society had to live an agricultural life to carry out the cultural mission (Genesis1:28). The Bible did not view agrarian culture itself as unfavorable.

But the Fall put humankind under Satan's authority. Afterward, the farming culture changed itself into an atheistic one. Humanity lived an agricultural life for survival (Genesis 3:23), not for the Creative purpose.

Immediately after the Fall, however, God promised Redemption with the Protoevangelium (Genesis 3:15). From then on, two groups made up one humanity: believers in future Redemption and unbelievers.

The believers began to live a nomadic life, hoping for future redemption, whereas the unbelievers – an agricultural experience for present survival on earth.

Anthropological sociology allegedly says that the emergence of both cultures required lots of time. However, the Primeval History of the Bible records that agriculture developed earlier than nomad, and nomadic lives began after the Fall.

Nomadic culture well helped the believers to serve as the salt and light of the world. On the contrary, God always destroyed whosoever to give up the role.

The New Testament had ended the role of Canaan's land and the Old Testament's nomadic culture. However, the teachings and lessons of nomadic culture remained in Christian thought, philosophy, and values. Jesus himself claimed that the saints, living a nomadic life of faith, could be the light and salt of the world.

In 313 AD, Christianity officially became a national religion. Since then, it has become one of the cultural mainstreams in Europe. The problem was that the regime of that time used Christianity as a means and method of governing the world. The Byzantine Empire was not different from the Davidic Dynasty of the Old Testament times. The Empire was not biblical.

The creation story or the Primeval History did not claim that this world would become the Kingdom of God. The Divine Dominion certainly exists spiritually among the nations in this world. The kingdom of God will reveal its actual appearance only after the last judgment by fire.

For the time being, the Kingdom of God cannot be the dominant principle of the world. Paradoxically, the Kingdom of God is the central theme of the Bible, but an invisible reality. Therefore, the Christian life of faith has to be fundamentally nomadic.

Nomads live on the outskirts of the village. They make a living in exchange for products with the villagers but not join the mainstream. Nevertheless, the villagers cannot ignore nomads. Abraham had 318 trained servants, born in his own house. The patriarchs were strong enough to make equal covenants with the Gentile kings. However, they always lived far from the village, not in its center.

Canaanite geopolitics also testifies well to it. Canaan was located in the middle of the world and always open to the outside. However, Israel ever had to live a closed nomadic life inside Canaan with scarce agricultural land. And also, shepherding life could not get along with farming life even in Canaan.

This nomadic life of faith continues in the New Testament times. But this type of faith life turned into personal values of believers in the Divine Creation and Redemption. They live a nomadic life of faith in the spiritual form. By doing it, they act as the light and salt of the world.

Fundamentally, the nomadic life of faith is not a power or principle to govern the world. On the one hand, this life of faith interacts with the world but, on the other hand, avoids it.

It does not mean the unconditional exclusion to abandon the belongings to the world or the willing compromise to accept it. The nomadic saints, living as an outsider, interact with the world and simultaneously distinguish themselves from it.

Such believers are always ready to alienate themselves from the world. In short, true believers willingly enjoy this social alienation and solitude. They are prepared to give up Christianity's earnest desire to become the dominant power of society.

It is because the nomadic life of faith fundamentally takes into consideration a spiritual battle. Physical force cannot overcome this struggle. Believers must be satisfied to serve personally as the world's light and salt by a nomadic life of faith.

Finally, Primeval History argues that it is impossible to separate religion, theology, and faith from history, society, and ethics. Furthermore, it teaches that they ultimately determine the life and fate of individuals and society.

In short, Primeval History was like a manual or instruction on how to live a godly life in the world to achieve the eventual purpose of God's Creation. The diagram below illustrates it well.

	Creator	Satan
religion	Jehovah	Baal
worship	Truth and spirit	idolatry
worldview	eschatological/time	hedonism/space
theology	creationism	Atheism
thinking	Faith/future world	reason/present world
life	Unsettled nomadic/ natural protection	Settled agrarian/ natural contamination
society	individualism/horizontal	totalitarian/vertical
wealth	In Heaven	On earth
politics	Rule by God's law/ democracy/peace	Rule by men's virtues/ authoritarian/chaos
rulership	Shepherd to serve all men	Conqueror to be served by all men
ethics	love	violence

The ignorant or negligent of God, the Creator, becomes athe

ist. He sees what is visible or visual, firmly believing its eternity. The visible world is a material one occupying space. To be obsessed with it, in other words, is to be dominated by space. There is no biblical understanding of the world subject to time.

An atheist naturally becomes a materialist. He sees world culture and history phenomenally. Ideas, philosophies, and systems of value become based on atheism.

Atheism had developed into various theisms. Deism and pantheism neutralize God the Creator because the first asserts only divine transcendence but the second – divine immanence.

And dualism sees the good and evil gods equally, weakening God, the Creator. All of them are different names of atheism. Humans come to feel free only by ignoring the existence of God, the Creator. It is what the Fall of the Bible taught. However, an atheist makes idols instead of God the Creator.

Only the Christian Bible records God the Creator. The Bible argues that religion cannot separate from history and culture. However, modern anthropologists assert that only in primitive times, religion and culture became one. Today the Bible's creationism is still ignored. Nevertheless, some believers insist on the creative faith of the Christian Bible.

Even today, there happen ideological quarrels and struggles between them. They are other names of a spiritual and theological battle. Understanding this well, the apostle Paul said that saints wage fighting, not by flesh and blood, but by ideology (Ephes.6:12). Even today, there is no separation between theology and human sociology.

"And you [hath he quickened], who were dead in trespas ses and sins; Wherein in time past ye walked according to t he course of this world, according to the prince of the pow er of the air, the spirit that now worketh in the children of di sobedience:" (Ephes.2:1-2)

"Wherefore remember, that ye [being] in time past Gentil es in the flesh, who are called Uncircumcision by that whic h is called the Circumcision in the flesh made by hands; Th at at that time ye were without Christ, being aliens from the commonwealth of Israel, and strangers from the covenants of promise, having no hope, and without God in the world: But now in Christ Jesus ye who sometimes were far off are made nigh by the blood of Christ." (Ephes.2:11-13)

The Primeval History (Genesis 1-11) recorded that believers in Creation and Redemption looked at the world from an eschat ological perspective. Meanwhile, unbelievers glanced at the wor ld from a materialistic view.

The theological or ideological difference between them is lik e the difference between time and space. Culturally, it is like the difference between nomadic life and agricultural life. Politically, i t is like the difference between democracy and authoritarianism. And religiously, it is the difference between Jehovah, the Creato r, and Baal, the agricultural god.

Abraham and Jacob, and later Israel, respectively, escaped f rom farming civilizations to live in Canaan, the promised land. T hey had to live as nomads in Canaan.

In the New-Testamental era, agrarian culture came to domin ate the world. Saints live in a Canaan-like world. And they are s piritually similar to nomads in the world.

Primitive history records that only devout believers, living a n omadic life of faith, were turned out to be the victors. He lived w orldly life as a citizen of God's Kingdom. In the New Testament t imes, it will be the secret to spiritual victory for nomad-like saint s.

"Therefore take no thought, saying, What shall we eat? o r, What shall we drink? or, Wherewithal shall we be clothed? (For after all these things do the Gentiles seek:) for your he avenly Father knoweth that ye have need of all these things. But seek ye first the kingdom of God, and his righteousnes s; and all these things shall be added unto you. Take theref ore no thought for the morrow: for the morrow shall take th ought for the things of itself. Sufficient unto the day [is] the evil thereof." (Mathew6:31-34)

Made in the USA
Monee, IL
15 November 2020